50 THRIFTY BIG ISLAND RESTAURANTS

Dining On A Budget, Local-Style

Dining On A Budget, Local-Style

Jessica Ferracane

WATERMARK
PUBLISHING

Design and illustrations
Leo Gonzalez

Production and maps
Julie Chun

Library of Congress Control Number: 2004108935

ISBN: 0-9742672-8-7

Watermark Publishing
1088 Bishop Street, Suite 310
Honolulu, Hawai'i 96813
Telephone: 1-808-587-7766
Toll-free 1-866-900-BOOK

e-mail: sales@bookshawaii.net
Web site: www.bookshawaii.net

Printed in the United States of America

To my husband, Steve, whose photos, input and appetite appear throughout these pages

Jessica Ferracane

Contents

Acknowledgments

Mahalo nui loa to all the local folks who completed my survey or gave me word-of-mouth (literally!) suggestions on the thriftiest, most delicious Big Island dining options. Without you, this book would have not been possible. Thank you to Andrea Hennings, whose home-grown knowledge of Kona helped me immensely. Another big mahalo to my patient publisher, George Engebretson of Watermark Publishing. And a special mahalo to the Big Island restaurateurs who realize that fabulous, innovative cuisine doesn't always come with a big fat price tag. *Bon apetít!*

Foreword
by Brian Berry

If you're a seasoned traveler, you may already be armed with Hawai'i guidebooks and magazine articles you've saved in planning your trip. But what you're probably missing is a local's perspective on where to eat well at reasonable prices. The Big Island of Hawai'i is part of the U.S., of course, but you'll be pleasantly surprised at how exotic and unfamiliar it can be. On the other hand, many a tourist has been found walking in a daze, shell-shocked, after spending two days' vacation money on one meal and drinks at one of our excellent four-star resorts.

Want to experience the true flavor of the Big Island without busting your wallet? Then you need *50 Thrifty Big Island Restaurants*, cleverly written by Jessica Ferracane. Jessica, who was raised in the Islands, has first-hand knowledge of local foods. And as the food and travel writer for *Hawai'i Island Journal*, I can vouch for the fact that she has done her homework—eating her way through all the restaurants listed in this guide. From a tiny Thai restaurant hidden in Hilo to a roadside fruit stand serving gourmet sandwiches in Nā'ālehu to a Waimea café that specializes in the local breakfast favorite, Loco Moco, this valuable handbook covers the entire island. Local residents will also find it helpful when they visit unfamiliar communities.

The time, money and hunger pangs you can save yourself by using this little book will surprise you. Have fun, and good eating!

Introduction

Hawai'i's Big Island offers so much to do: you can really work up an appetite by surfing, training for the Ironman triathlon, swimming, scuba diving and snorkeling, horseback riding, exploring the world's most active volcano, pig hunting, or hiking through waterfall-rich jungles and sun-scorched petroglyph fields. It's a good thing there are quality calories to be consumed on this fine island, with all these activities helping to burn them off. The trick is knowing where to eat well, without breaking the bank.

We are a very *big* island, and thrifty dining options can be hard to find. Notable and thrifty are even harder to find, so I've done your homework for you, dear reader. Whether you're a first-time Big Island visitor, or a born-and-bred local from Hilo who wants to know where to eat in Kealakekua or if that new place in town is any good, this book has 50 tasty suggestions for you.

I like to think I know a thing or two about food, having worked in Hawai'i as a food server, a journalist and co-author of *50 Thrifty Maui Restaurants*, and now as a public relations professional at a luxury resort known for its fine cuisine. The truth is, eating out is a learning experience. I've walked away from dirty kitchens and steered clear of mediocrity, chain establishments and overrated, overpriced restaurants. I offer you instead my honest recommendations for inexpensive, memorable and, in some cases, authentically local cuisine. If there's a great view—bonus!

So what's thrifty? You need to be able to eat breakfast or lunch for $10 per person, including tip and tax. Dinner should be no more than $20 per person, preferably less. Many restaurants within these pages fall well below these criteria; some are right there.

And while I like to think I know the Big Island dining scene like the back of my fork, the reality is that I might have missed a real gem along the way, so I welcome your "feed"back for future editions. Write to me at Watermark Publishing, 1088 Bishop Street,

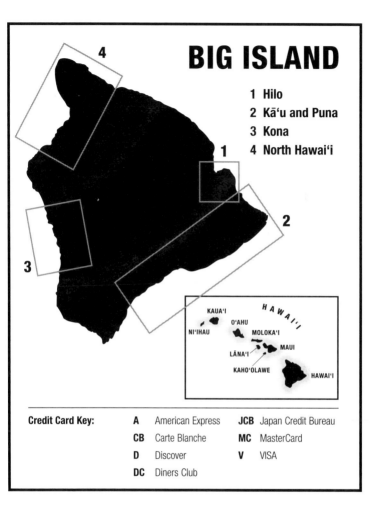

BIG ISLAND

1 Hilo
2 Kāʻu and Puna
3 Kona
4 North Hawaiʻi

HAWAIʻI

KAUAʻI
NIʻIHAU
OʻAHU
MOLOKAʻI
LĀNAʻI
KAHOʻOLAWE
MAUI
HAWAIʻI

Credit Card Key:

A	American Express	JCB	Japan Credit Bureau
CB	Carte Blanche	MC	MasterCard
D	Discover	V	VISA
DC	Diners Club		

Suite 310, Honolulu, Hawaiʻi, 96813, or drop me an email at
50thrifty@earthlink.net.
Let's eat!

Jessica Ferracane

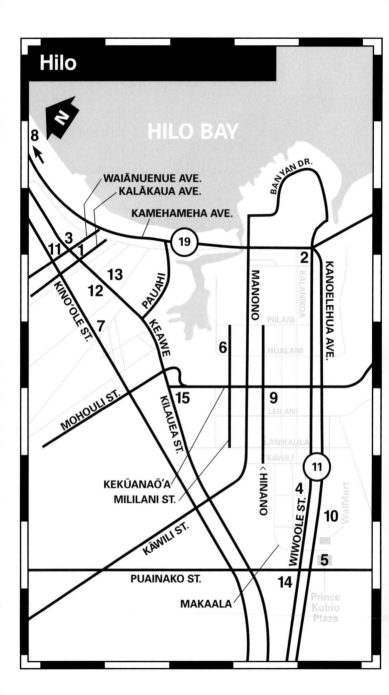

Hilo Restaurants

Breakfast
1. Bears' Coffee
2. Ken's House of Pancakes
3. Restaurant Kaikodo

Lunch
4. Blane's Drive Inn
5. Maui Tacos
6. Miyo's
7. O'Keefe & Sons Bread Bakers
8. What's Shakin'

Dinner
9. Don's Grill
10. Hilo Bay Café
11. Island Cantina
12. Naung Mai Thai Kitchen
13. Ocean Sushi Deli
14. Pizza Hawaii & Deli
15. Restaurant Miwa

CUISINE	**Homemade pastries and espresso bar**
LOCATION	**Downtown Hilo, on Keawe Street**
HOURS	**Breakfast: Monday-Friday, 7 a.m. to 11:30 a.m.; lunch: Monday-Friday, 10:30 a.m. to 2:30 p.m.; Saturday, 7 a.m. to 1 p.m.; Sunday, 8 a.m. to noon**
SEATING	**30 inside, about 10 outside**
PARKING	**Ample public parking along the street or in the public lot at Keawe and Waiānuenue streets**
OPENED	**1993**
ALCOHOL	**No**
PLASTIC	**Cash or check only**

Bears' Coffee
106 Keawe Street, Hilo
Telephone 935-0708

The first thing I noticed about this popular cafe on Keawe street is its eclectic crowd. Once I slipped past the bunch of regulars: Vietnam vets, attorneys, surfers, teenagers, writers and other assorted beatniks, I was surprised to discover a really tasty breakfast menu. Now I'm just another face in the morning crowd.

Bears' offers breakfast and lunch; both are good. For breakfast, I get the Big Bad Buster, which is one egg cooked with ham, spinach and cheddar cheese, plus an English muffin, for only $4.25. If I'm in the mood for fruit and granola, I have a parfait of plain yogurt sprinkled with granola and topped with fresh papaya, apple banana, strawberries and blueberries. At $4.25, these sell out, so plan on going early. Bears' also serves unbelievably great bagel meals ($1.45 to $6.75), a mean Bear Paw ($2.50), a killer Cinnamon Roll ($2.25) and affordable coffee drinks. Coffee is $1.50; lattes are $2.75; a mocha, the most expensive of their specialty coffee and espresso drinks, is $3.

Toto, we're not in Starbucks anymore...

CUISINE **Any and every kine!**

LOCATION **Ken's is a landmark, at the corner of Kamehameha and Kanoelehua avenues (the junction of State Highways 19 and 11, respectively.)**

HOURS **Daily, 24 hours**

SEATING **180, including 11 stools at the counter**

PARKING **Parking lot out front**

OPENED **1971**

ALCOHOL **No**

PLASTIC **A, DC, D, MC, V**

NOTES **The only time Ken's closes is for the annual employee holiday party.**

Ken's House of Pancakes
1730 Kamehameha Avenue, Hilo
Telephone 935-8711

Ken's House of Pancakes is the best restaurant in Hilo, according to veteran waitress Irene, a bundle of beautiful energy who has worked there for 30 years and who twice has been voted "Best Waitress" in East Hawai'i by readers of the *Hawaii Tribune-Herald*. Irene knows a thing or two.

Like what to order. Like any self-respecting local girl, I like to eat saimin for breakfast occasionally. At Ken's, the saimin is made with fresh Hilo-made Maebo Noodles and an imported shrimp broth that separates this saimin from the rest of the pack. Irene steered me toward the Keiki Min, a "small" portion for $3.75. Floating on the surface of the broth, above a submerged bed of dense noodles, are scrambled egg, a few slices of char siu pork and a pink-and-white slice of fish cake. I slurp mine down with a dollop of the sinus-clearing Chinese hot mustard served on the side. Whoa, baby!

The Keiki Min leaves enough room to try one single namesake pancake ($1.75 a la carte). This is pancake perfection, with a thin, crispy edge and plenty of butter and syrup, including maple and coconut. Breakfast of champions!

Ken's is open 24 hours a day and is a welcome stop for everyone, from cops to late-night party animals to volcano observers headed back home or back to their hotels.

CUISINE	**Upscale "East meets Island West"**
LOCATION	**Historic downtown Hilo, on the corner of Keawe and Waianuenue streets**
WEB	**www.restaurantkaikodo.com**
HOURS	**Sunday brunch: 10:30 a.m.-2:30 p.m.; lunch: 11 a.m. to 2:30 p.m., Monday-Saturday; dinner: 5 p.m. to 9:30 p.m., Sunday-Thursday; 5 p.m.-10 p.m., Friday and Saturday; bar open all day till closing**
SEATING	**90 in the main dining room; additional facilities available**
PARKING	**Public parking lot across the street; public stalls usually abundant in downtown Hilo**
OPENED	**May 2003**
ALCOHOL	**Full bar**
PLASTIC	**A, MC, V, JCB**
NOTES	**The Hilo Museum of Art and Culture, with exhibition, concert and recital hall facilities is slated to occupy the refurbished second floor in 2005.**

Restaurant Kaikodo
60 Keawe Street, Hilo
Telephone 961-2558

A few of the restaurants profiled in this book have elevated the Big Island dining scene to new heights, and Kaikodo tops the list. While not all Kaikodo's prices fit into the thrifty category, it's not impossible to get a memorable meal at an affordable price, especially if you duck in for Sunday brunch.

This is no gorge-fest Sunday buffet. Expect instead a rather elegant menu offering items like Smoked 'Ahi Paté ($5) or the Kaikodo Chicken Salad, with romaine, Farmer's Market tangerines, toasted almonds, avocado and tomato in a tangy lemon-lime vinaigrette ($11). I nearly heeded my inner supermodel and ordered it, but instead I tore into the Kaikodo Brunch Special, which is two poached eggs perched on a bed of house-made roast beef hash and sliced tomato, topped with chili pepper hollandaise. It includes a tropical fruit salad, and get this: an ice cream sundae for dessert, plus coffee, tea or orange juice, for only $15. Who can blame me? It's just enough to share between two hungry supermodels.

Restaurant Kaikodo has been praised in national food magazines for its design as well as its noteworthy cuisine. The restaurant is located in a renovated turn-of-the-century building in downtown Hilo and was designed by the owners, who have devoted a lifetime to the arts. It exudes a casual Asian elegance with its sky-high ceilings, innovative lighting, and my favorite ladies' room on the island, featuring blue glass sink bowls and cool glass art.

CUISINE	**Local-style**
LOCATION	**Industrial Hilo, near Big Island Honda**
HOURS	**Monday-Saturday, 5 a.m. to 9 p.m.; Sunday, 6 a.m. to 9 p.m.**
SEATING	**56**
PARKING	**Parking lot**
OPENED	**1991 at the Wiwoole location**
ALCOHOL	**No**
PLASTIC	**MC, V**
NOTES	**There's another location in downtown Hilo, at 217 Wainuenue Avenue; their number is 969-9494.**

Blane's Drive Inn
150 Wiwoole Street, Hilo
Telephone 935-2259; Fax 935-2557

Blane's must be one of the thriftiest restaurants on the entire Big Island, if not the absolute winner. Prices range from $1.60 for a simple hamburger to $7 for a full Mahi Mahi plate lunch. And that's just a sample of Blane's massive menu, which has something for just about everyone—and most items, including the dressings, are homemade.

I'm sold on Blane's Chili and Rice, which is the best I've tried on the Island yet. For a mere $2.75, you get a big Styrofoam container of chili, simmered slowly with fresh hamburger, kidney beans, chili powder, onions and other ingredients that I could not coax out of owner Blane Aburamen for love or money. On the bottom, lots of white sticky rice, which is how real locals eat their chili.

Blane's personal favorite is the crispy Chicken Katsu, which is the Japanese version of the American classic, fried chicken, using panko breadcrumbs instead of flour as the coating. It's really 'ono, and it's only $3.75 for a bowl with rice, or $6.75 for a deluxe plate, which includes two scoops of rice, macaroni salad and heart-healthy miso soup. Broke da mout'!

One caveat: I go to the Industrial location, near Big Island Honda, where the lines are always long. Call and order in advance, or expect *slow* fast food.

CUISINE	**Mexican-American**
LOCATION	**Prince Kuhio Plaza, Hilo**
WEB	**www.mauitacos.com**
HOURS	**Monday-Thursday, 9 a.m. to 7 p.m.; Saturday, 9 a.m. to 9 p.m.; Sunday, 9 a.m. to 6 p.m.**
SEATING	**40**
PARKING	**Plenty of parking at the mall**
OPENED	**1996**
ALCOHOL	**Beer and wine available**
PLASTIC	**V, M, JCB, DC, A**

Maui Tacos
111 E. Puainako Street, Hilo
Telephone 959-0359

When I want a taste of Maui, I don't head to the airport; I go to Prince Kuhio Mall in Hilo for a little "Mauitude."

I lived in Lahaina for 10 years and used to eat at all four Maui Tacos locations on the Valley Isle before moving to the Big Island a few years ago. I was pleasantly surprised to stumble upon the Hilo store while shopping one afternoon.

While my favorite is the Lahaina Surf burrito (a massive flour tortilla filled with jack and cheddar cheese, rice, guacamole, fresh salsa and steak or chicken, $6.95), I only had a $5 bill, so I opted for the thriftier Maui Taco. The Maui Taco is a double-soft-shell tortilla with black or pinto beans. A no-frills protein fix, but you can peel the shells apart to make two tacos, for a mere $3.50. (I looked longingly at the Tecate beer but couldn't justify spending more money on a beer than my food.) Tip: the complimentary salsa bars at Maui Tacos are loaded with all kinds of extras, like jalapeños, chopped cilantro and different house-made salsas. I usually doctor my taco with my favorite, owner/chef Mark Ellman's Pineapple Passion salsa, made with Hawaiian pineapple, tomatillos, garlic, cilantro, sweet onion, jalapeno, lime juice and lots of aloha. *Olé!*

Chef Mark has seven Maui Tacos restaurants in Hawaii and seven on the mainland, plus his fantastic Penne Pasta Cafe in Lahaina. Save room for Mauitude!

CUISINE	**Homestyle Japanese**
LOCATION	**Waiakea Villas Hotel**
HOURS	**Monday-Saturday: lunch, 11 a.m. to 2 p.m.; dinner, 5:30 p.m. to 8:30 p.m.; closed Sundays**
SEATING	**60**
PARKING	**Ample parking out front**
OPENED	**1986**
ALCOHOL	**BYOB**
PLASTIC	**V, MC**

Miyo's
400 Hualani Street, Hilo
Telephone 935-2273

Miyo's is one of those places you won't know exists unless you're a local or you get lucky. Tucked into the middle of the Waiakea Villas Hotel, at the mauka end of the Wailoa River State Park, Miyo's is off the beaten path, but you can't get lost. Just head mauka from the airport road (Kekuanaoa Street), take a right on Miilani Street, and enter the Waiakea Villas on the left. Veer right, and you'll see a sign for a karaoke bar. Miyo's is right behind the bar, on the waterfront, up a steep flight of stairs.

Inside, the dining room overlooks the beautiful Waiakea Pond. High ceilings and the open kitchen create an inviting ambience, but it's the menu that keeps locals coming back. There are more than 50 enticing items to choose from. My server suggested the most popular: Tempura & Sesame Chicken ($8.50, served with rice, salad, miso soup and Japanese pickles). A massive platter arrived in minutes, complete with a Farmer's Market-fresh salad. The chicken—cubed, deep-fried and sprinkled with sesame seeds—was marvelously crisp and delicious, and not the least bit greasy; same for the vegetable tempura. My writer pal Lisa had Tempura and Sashimi (the latter fresh-caught by local fishermen) and her mom enjoyed the Beef Teriyaki and Sashimi plate (each $8.75). Normally I taste all the food on the table, but we munched away our selections before I got the chance.

Miyo's ranks among my top ten favorite Big Island places, and I look forward to exploring the menu further in the future.

CUISINE   **Bakery-fresh café specialties**

LOCATION   **Across the street from the *Hawaii Tribune-Herald* newspaper building**

HOURS   **Monday-Friday, 6 a.m. to 5 p.m.; Saturday; 6 a.m. to 3 p.m.; closed Sunday**

SEATING   **Around 20, inside and outside**

PARKING   **Several spaces in front; parking can be a challenge during lunch hours**

OPENED   **1998**

ALCOHOL   **No**

PLASTIC   **A, JCB, MC, V**

NOTES   **You can also get O'Keefe's breads at many stores and the Hilo Farmer's Market on Wednesdays and Saturdays.**

O'Keefe & Sons Bread Bakers
347 Kinoole Street, Hilo
Telephone 934-9334

The plain building that houses O'Keefe's bakery provides no hint of the wondrous creations rising inside, unless you're passing by and catch a whiff.

There are the standard sweet pastries, rolls and countless varieties of irresistible loaves, but for a real treat, plan on Monday or Friday lunch. On Mondays, amazing, thick, locally grown-sweet corn chowder, served in a fresh-baked roasted garlic sourdough bread bowl, is the *pièce de resistance*. On Fridays, it's a marvelous New England clam chowder bowl. Both are $5.95, with a small green salad. Make sure you ask for a few pats of complimentary, ultra-gourmet Plugra butter to spread on the leftover "bowl." I almost always get the soup special, but I also like the Chicken Macadamia Nut Salad Sandwich on rye ($5.25) and the Mini Sausage Rolls baked with apples and mustard, $1.75 each.

Owner Jim O'Keefe is a former New Englander and the son of a prominent East Coast baker, who helped his dad by eating his products. Jim came to the Big Island on vacation 35 years ago and never looked back. Nowadays, he's eaten his way to the top of the Big Island food chain, supplying many resorts, grocery stores and the Hilo Farmer's Market with his fine baked goods.

CUISINE **Fresh fruit smoothies and healthy, creative entrées**

LOCATION **On the Four-Mile Scenic Route off Highway 19 (Old Māmalahoa Hwy.), two miles past the Hawai'i Tropical Botanical Garden, towards Honoka'a**

HOURS **Daily, 10 a.m. to 5 p.m. (5:30 p.m. in summer)**

SEATING **About 30, on picnic tables and on the lanai**

PARKING **Parking area in front**

OPENED **1995**

ALCOHOL **No**

PLASTIC **MC, V**

NOTE **Most of the fruit is grown on the owners' Onomea farm.**

What's Shakin'
27-999 Old Māmalahoa Highway, Pepeʻekeo
Telephone 964-3080

This charming little plantation-style lunch cottage is so cute you'll want to reach out and pinch its cheeks. Since it doesn't have any, pull over and get some lunch instead.

But before you climb the steps, turn around and take in the scenery. Dazzling ocean views framed by verdant, lush Hawaiian rainforest and rolling green lawns give customers a gorgeous view. If you're en route to the Hawaiʻi Tropical Botanical Garden (a must-see) along the Four-Mile Scenic Route, this is an ideal place to grab a bite. What's Shakin' marks the beginning (or the end) of one of Hawaiʻi's most beautiful drives.

The menu board features an array of healthy, enticing choices. Try the Southwestern Chicken Wrap: a bakery-fresh herb tortilla rolled with black beans, white-meat chicken and home-made salsa ($7.95). They melt cheddar cheese into the tortilla to keep it from falling apart—genius! Entrées are served with fresh exotic fruit grown on the owners' farm. My wrap came with strawberry papaya, white guava and soursop, an aromatic, juicy white-fleshed fruit I'd never seen before. I love scrumptious surprises!

The fresh fruit smoothies are superb, with no added sugar, and are worth the price, $4.45 medium, $5.15 large. There are all kinds of things to try and buy, from the Teriyaki Ginger Tempeh Burger ($6.95) to Hawaiian plants, delicious freaky fruit and fresh-baked goodies like pineapple muffins and coconut pie. You'll be glad you stopped.

CUISINE **Local and homestyle diner food**

LOCATION **A few blocks mauka of the Hilo International Airport intersection, on the same street as Big Island Candies**

HOURS **Closed Monday; Tuesday-Thursday, 10:30 a.m. to 9 p.m.; Friday, 10:30 a.m. to 10 p.m.; Saturday and Sunday, 10 a.m. to 9 p.m.**

SEATING **76**

PARKING **Parking lot available**

OPENED **1988**

ALCOHOL **Beer and wine, from $2.75**

PLASTIC **A, MC, V**

NOTES **Don's Grill also operates a popular catering business.**

Don's Grill
485 Hinano Street, Hilo
Telephone 935-9099

I had a few friends beg me not to put Don's Grill in this book. They want to keep it all for themselves, like a hidden beach or favorite surf spot. "It's already busy enough," they pleaded. But after testing the waters myself, I decided it wouldn't be fair not to share.

The house special is a super-succulent, perfectly seasoned rotisserie half-chicken, which comes with a nice green salad, a choice of rice, mashed potatoes or fries, and a drink for only $7.95. One person can get a full homestyle dinner for less than $10—which could make it the thriftiest dinner choice in this book and qualifies it as a personal favorite. I've also been known to splurge on a Don's cheddar cheeseburger ($5.25, including fries). The lunch and dinner menus are the same, but the prices go up a notch at dinner to include the salad, carbs and drink.

Owner Don Ho'ota is the chief cook, and he also makes a variety of homemade pies ($2.25 a slice). Hungry locals crowd in for lunch and dinner, but visitors are welcome. Check out the famous Big Island Candies factory just down Hinano Street, then head to Don's for a bite. You'll like Don's Grill's homey, almost diner-like ambience, clean kitchen, and prompt, friendly service. But don't tell anyone. It'll be our secret.

CUISINE	**Eclectic American**
LOCATION	**Near Office Max at the WalMart shopping center**
HOURS	**Daily, lunch: 11 a.m. to 2 p.m.; dinner: 5 p.m. to 9 p.m.; bar open 2 p.m. to 5 p.m.**
SEATING	**60**
PARKING	**Sufficient parking at the shopping center**
OPENED	**October 2003**
ALCOHOL	**Full bar**
PLASTIC	**A, D, MC, V**
NOTES	**The owner also has Island Naturals Market & Deli across the parking lot.**

Hilo Bay Café
315 Makaala Street, Hilo
Telephone 935-4939

Don't let its unglamorous strip mall location fool you—Hilo Bay Café is as sleek as a San Francisco hot spot, with black lacquer furniture, a stylishly modern interior and, best of all, remarkably creative cuisine at a great price.

The menu is astounding: some items like the Beet Salad with Grilled Haloumi Cheese, tossed with applewood-smoked bacon and organic micro-greens, go for as little as $6. Vegan garlic fries are tempting at $3, but I get the salad instead, and then the house-made vegan Pot Pie for my entrée, a savory stew of fresh vegetables baked in the best flaky crust I've tasted ($8). The Roasted Chicken Breast ($14) is Atkins-friendly, stuffed with pine nuts and garlic cream cheese and served on wilted spinach with smoked bacon. Scrumptious!

"We want everyone to be able to dine, no matter what's in their wallet," says Chef Joshua. Almost everything is organic, the meats are all natural, and every single dish I've had there has deserved applause. Also applause worthy is the motto printed at the bottom of the menu: *At the heart of our food is the belief that local and organic ingredients are better for the earth and you.*

Check out the fine wine list ($7/glass), the grilled Rib Eye Pepper Steak ($17) and the house-made Ravioli ($12), and be sure to save room for the seasonal Fresh Fruit Tart, $6 (see Sweet Endings).

CUISINE	**Mexican/Southwestern**
LOCATION	**Adjacent to the Kalākaua Park, across from the East-West Cultural Center**
HOURS	**Daily, 11 a.m. to 9 p.m.**
SEATING	**50**
PARKING	**Public stalls available**
OPENED	**2002**
ALCOHOL	**BYOB for now**
PLASTIC	**V, MC, JCB, DC, D**
NOTES	**Formerly called Hawaiian Jungle, it reopened under new ownership in March 2004.**

Island Cantina
110 Kalākaua Street, Hilo
Telephone 969-7009

My husband Steve and I had a bad case of cabin fever one Sunday afternoon and decided to go tripping around downtown Hilo. We wound up at Island Cantina, a happening Mexican joint adjacent to Kalākaua Park.

Bright Mexican blankets, covered in clear plastic, serve as tablecloths. It's a very colorful, inviting place with very colorful, inviting chips and salsa. Green, blue, yellow and red corn tortilla chips are served with a nut-free cilantro pesto and "cantina sauce" salsa, which has enough kick to say hello but not enough to feel at goodbye. We scarfed the chips and knocked back a half-order of Chicken Nachos ($5.95).

Joe, the man running the stoves, is also co-owner. He told us he used to operate the bubble machine on the Lawrence Welk Show. Evidently, Joe is multi-talented. We dove into his sizzling steak Fajita Platter ($13.95) with *mucho gusto*.

Steve ordered a delectable Taco Salad with chicken ($9.95), served in a fried tortilla bowl with house-made Maui Onion dressing. Some non-Mexican items also looked delicious: Goat Cheese Salad with Tequila Lime Dressing ($9.95), Blackened Pork Chops ($13.95) and the Fresh Fish Platter ($13.95). The owners purchase many ingredients at the Hilo Farmer's Market.

As we left, other diners poured in. There's often a line to get in for dinner, so go early. It'll leave time for a post-supper stroll around downtown Hilo.

CUISINE	**Thai**
LOCATION	**Behind Garden Exchange in Hilo**
HOURS	**Monday-Friday, lunch: 11 a.m. to 2 p.m.; Monday-Saturday, dinner: 5 p.m. to 9 p.m.; closed Sunday**
SEATING	**30; take-out and catering available**
PARKING	**Free public parking along Kīlauea Avenue and Mamo Street**
OPENED	**2000; new ownership**
ALCOHOL	**BYOB with a $2 charge for glasses**
PLASTIC	**MC, V**
NOTES	**Absolutely no MSG is used here.**

Naung Mai Thai Kitchen
86 Kīlauea Avenue, Hilo
Telephone 934-7540

My favorite foods burst with flavors but are low in fat, are full of fresh vegetables and fill me up. You'll find all of the above at Naung Mai Thai Kitchen in downtown Hilo.

Located two blocks up from the Hilo Farmer's Market, this small, clean, affordable and inviting restaurant attracts Hilo locals, visitors and even celebrities like Dennis Hopper.

I always order the spicy Cucumber Salad with julienne carrots, peanuts and tomatoes in a tantalizing hot pepper sauce. I can fantasize about visiting Thailand some day, all for $5.95. The Thai Spring Rolls appetizer ($6.95) is a rice wrapper packed with fresh mint, carrot and tofu, then sliced into tasty bite-size pieces, served with a sweet chili dipping sauce. The naughty Summer Rolls ($7.95) are deep-fried to a golden brown.

The last time I was in, my server steered me toward the medium-hot Yellow Curry with Shrimp entrée ($10.95), and I'm not sure I'll ever try anything else. This is an extraordinary curry, made with a zillion different spices, coconut milk, chunks of potato, carrots and big fat shrimp, served in a tureen with a side of jasmine rice. Heavenly! I left too full to indulge in my beloved ginger-flavored Hilo Homemade Ice Cream ($3 a scoop; see Sweet Endings) but fat and happy nonetheless.

CUISINE	**Sushi and sashimi**
LOCATION	**Downtown Hilo**
HOURS	**Monday-Saturday, lunch: 10 a.m. to 2 p.m.; dinner: 4:30 p.m. to 9 p.m.; closed Sunday**
SEATING	**45**
PARKING	**Parallel parking along Keawe Street**
OPENED	**June 1997**
ALCOHOL	**BYOB**
PLASTIC	**A, DC, D, JCB, MC, V**

Ocean Sushi Deli
239 Keawe Street, Hilo
Telephone 961-6625

Love sushi, but hate spendy sushi bar prices? Check out Ocean Sushi Deli the next time you're in downtown Hilo.

Located a stone's throw from the Hilo Farmer's Market and just a few blocks from the Suisan fish dock, Ocean Sushi parlays choice Big Island ingredients into mind-boggling sushi selections, some traditional, some downright freaky. Try the Banzai Natto Roll, a puckery mouthful of *natto* (fermented soybeans), 'ahi, cucumber, *ume* (pickled plum) and *kaiware* (radish sprouts), $4.50. I always order something new and something tried-and-true, like the Big Island Roll: fresh 'ahi, avocado, macadamia nuts and spicy mayo for $4.50, or the fresh 'ahi sashimi, $6.75 for seven pieces. You can BYOB, and we usually do. Pick up a six-pack of Japanese beer from the KTA grocery store just a few doors south.

There isn't much to see, unless you count the young denim-clad Japanese-American sisters who deftly handle the dining room alone. Diners get a kick out of watching them run back and forth across Keawe Street to Tsunami Grill (same owner), where they pick up tempura for their best guests.

Miso soup and steamed rice are a buck each, and sushi choices include nigiri, maki, inari, hosomaki, temaki and chirashi styles. You'll be challenged to find better, less expensive sushi on the Big Island.

CUISINE	**Homemade pizzas & deli**
LOCATION	**Puainako Center**
HOURS	**Monday-Thursday, 11 a.m. to 8:30 p.m.; Friday and Saturday, 11 a.m. to 9:30 p.m.; Sunday, 12 noon to 8 p.m.**
SEATING	**35, inside and outside**
PARKING	**Free parking at Puainako Center**
OPENED	**June 2003**
ALCOHOL	**No**
PLASTIC	**MC, V**

Pizza Hawaii and Deli
2100 Kanoelehua Avenue, Hilo
Telephone 959-9932

I used to whine that Hilo lacked good, thrifty pizza, but then George Poulos came along, a little over a year ago, and saved me. His wonderful Pizza Hawaii and Deli restaurant, in convenient Puainako Center, features great—and cheap!—fare, with homemade sauces, dough and French rolls.

Pizza Hawaii and Deli is open for lunch, too, but occasionally I like to grab a 19-inch pizza pie after work for an indulgent Friday night dinner. My husband eats the lion's share—I can put away three slices, then I'm done. We both love the crust: New York-style, more on the thin side, not one of those thick, doughy Chicago jobs. Our favorite is the California Gourmet, an irresistible pizza made with fresh homemade tomato sauce AND pesto, plus mozzarella, feta cheese, sun-dried tomatoes, garlic and green onions. It goes down well with red or white wine, a fine way to start the weekend.

The $1.90 individual slices are gargantuan, with toppings another 45 cents each. The best deal is the two-slice combo, $4.65 for plain cheese and a large drink. Toppings for both slices are an additional 75 cents.

This relative newcomer to the Puainako dining scene (I swear, there is one) also turns out remarkable sandwiches, served hot on a homemade French roll, like the Sausage and Peppers ($5.75). And be sure to try the Pizza Bakes, which George claims are better than calzones. I'll keep you posted.

CUISINE   **Traditional Japanese**

LOCATION **In the back corner of Hilo Shopping
          Center, at the intersection of Kekuanaoa
          and Kīlauea avenues**

HOURS   **Monday-Saturday, lunch: 11 a.m. to
          2 p.m.; dinner: 5 p.m. to 10 p.m.; Sunday,
          closed for lunch; dinner: 5 p.m. to 9 p.m.**

SEATING   **About 72, including eight seats at the
          sushi bar**

PARKING   **Ample parking at the shopping center**

OPENED   **1987**

ALCOHOL   **Full bar**

PLASTIC   **A, MC, V, DC, D, JCB**

NOTES   **Don't confuse this restaurant with
          Miyo's.**

Restaurant Miwa
1261 Kīlauea Avenue, Hilo
Telephone 961-4454

In Japanese, *miwa* means "beautiful" or "tasty" and *wa* means "peace," "harmony" or "cooking." No matter how you interpret it, Restaurant Miwa lives up to its name.

The master behind the sushi bar is Japan-born owner/chef Shige, a tireless sushi crusader who puts in about 16 hours a day creating *oishi* (delicious) Japanese food for his loyal local customers. He is at the Suisan fish dock every day at 7 a.m., hand-selecting fresh fish caught by the Hilo fishing fleet. He then shops the Hilo Farmer's Market for fresh produce, and the wasabi root he serves is imported fresh.

We love his sushi ($3 for a small California roll), the incredible fresh ahi sashimi (market price), and the mouthwatering fresh flounder, which is usually an Atlantic Ocean fish. But Miwa's flounder is farm-raised at the Natural Energy Labs of Hawaii (NELHA) in Kona, and Shige deep-fries it crisp, complete with bones, skin and tail, and serves it with pickled vegetables, rice, miso soup, tea and ponzu dipping sauce. Pluck the white, flaky meat off the bones with your chopsticks and eat the crunchy tail in one bite. Yum! Market price was $9.95 that night, and the rest of the menu (sushi, tempura, katsu, teriyaki, udon, etc.) is also affordable for lunch or dinner.

Restaurant Miwa serves ultra-fresh sushi and sashimi, as well as true Japanese delicacies like the Natto Roll, made with a fermented soybean paste, which I have avoided so far. Maybe next time!

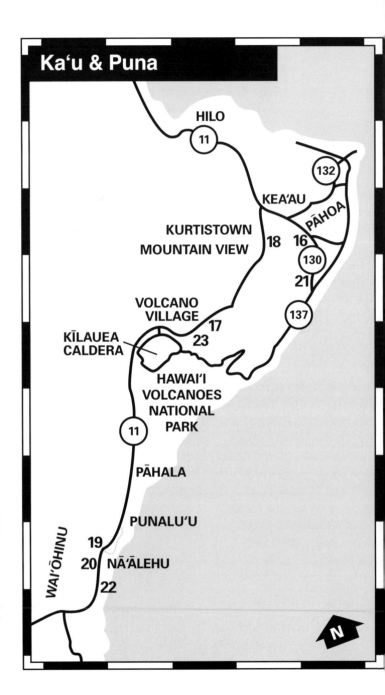

Ka'u & Puna

Ka'u & Puna

Breakfast

Lunch

Dinner

CUISINE	American with local flair
LOCATION	One block past the Post Office in "downtown" Pāhoa
HOURS	Daily, 7 a.m. to 9:30 p.m.; breakfast served until 11 a.m
SEATING	64 in the dining room; 24 in the lounge
PARKING	Free parking out front
OPENED	1997
ALCOHOL	Lounge serves a full bar; open daily from 7 a.m. to around 9:30 p.m.
PLASTIC	A, D, MC, V
NOTES	Breakfast, lunch and dinner are served, with affordable keiki menus.

Black Rock Cafe
15-2872 Government Main Road, Pāhoa
Telephone 965-1177

Pāhoa is largely unsung as a Big Island destination, but it's well worth the detour off Highway 11 onto Highway 130 towards Puna's coastal area, especially on a sunny day. This is where Pele's fiery path engulfed the town of Kalapana, where windswept black lava rock coastlines dominate, where mysterious *heiau* (temples) were built, and where diversified agriculture such as papayas, noni, and (ahem) other plants thrive.

And along the way, there's the humble Black Rock Cafe, which serves the average American breakfast at a below-average price.

Steve and I slid into a vinyl booth on a Sunday and ordered away. We polished off a half-order of Homemade Biscuits and Sausage Gravy (good, especially for $2.50); tried a "short stack" of two mammoth pancakes ($2.95, better than most); then moved onto our breakfast entrees. I had the Florentine Omelet, three eggs filled with spinach, cheese and sour cream, for $4.95 (gotta love these prices); and Steve inhaled two over-medium eggs and bacon for $4.95. All egg dishes come with toast and rice or hash browns. The coffee is decent, and it's only $1.

By the way we gorged ourselves, you'd think we had inhaled some of Pāhoa's other agriculture, but that wasn't the case. We simply fueled up and spent the rest of the sunny morning exploring Kaimū to Cape Kumukahi by car, feasting our eyes on the rugged, yet beautiful, scenery.

CUISINE	**Italian, with some American items like Rib Eye Steak**
LOCATION	**Volcano Village, between the general store and the post office**
HOURS	**Daily, lunch: noon to 2:30 p.m.; dinner: 5:30 p.m. to 9:30 p.m.; closed Wednesdays**
SEATING	**About 50 total, inside and outside**
PARKING	**Parking in front and alongside**
OPENED	**2002**
ALCOHOL	**BYOB at press time, but getting their liquor license**
PLASTIC	**MC, JCB, V**
NOTE	**It's located in the space formerly occupied by Sert's restaurant.**

17

Kiawe Kitchen
19-4005 Old Volcano Road, Volcano Village
Telephone 967-7711

Don't let Kiawe Kitchen's menu prices stick in your slippah like one long, sharp kiawe thorn, brah. Sure, there are $22 Rib Eye Steaks, cracker-flat Italian-style brick oven pizzas and other slightly spendy specials that change daily, but you can safely tiptoe around those. What you want here is the Linguine alla Puttanesca.

Puttanesca lovers, stand up and be counted. Actually, pull out your wallets and count out $14, plus change, because that's how much this lusty, robusty pasta will set you back. I'm about half Italian, but my grandfather Ferracane never told me the meaning of the word "*puttanesca*," a derivative of the Italian word for whore. No wonder he never mentioned it!

Puttanesca is an Italian sauce made with fresh tomatoes, onions, capers, anchovies (you heard me), black olives, garlic, oregano and olive oil. The anchovies give the sauce a subtly pungent back-flavor that lingers like caviar on the taste buds. Apparently, the ladies who worked Italy's red-light districts made this dish for their prurient patrons. That was their business, but it's now our pleasure.

Whatever the case, the cooks at Kiawe Kitchen meld these ingredients into one of the most outstanding puttanesca sauces I've had the privilege of eating. Start with the always-delicious Soup of the Day ($5) and you'll be singing "Roxanne" in no time. Finish with a strong $3.75 latte, then step out into the cool Volcano evening. Grampy would have loved it.

CUISINE	Vietnamese/Thai/Chinese
LOCATION	Keaau Shopping Center
HOURS	Monday-Saturday, 10 a.m. to 9 p.m.; Sunday, noon to 9 p.m.
SEATING	50
PARKING	Ample parking at Keaau Shopping Center
OPENED	2000
ALCOHOL	BYOB
PLASTIC	MC, V

18

Lemongrass Restaurant
16-586 Old Volcano Road, Keaau
Telephone/Fax 982-8558

Lemongrass Restaurant has a loyal following of Asian food devotees in the Puna District as well as a fan base of visitors who are lucky enough to stumble upon it en route to or from Hawai'i Volcanoes National Park.

For dinner, owner/chef Fa Ye creates a flavorful fusion of Vietnamese, Thai and Chinese selections. The chef and owner of another locally acclaimed restaurant recommended I try the Tom Yum King soup, a hot and spicy coconut milk soup with lots of plump shrimp and vegetables ($8.95, dinner only). I wish I'd discovered it sooner, because Lemongrass is only a few miles from our Mountainview cabin. Tom Yum King is now our favorite

entrée there, with a strong, slightly savage kick to it. The not-too-thick broth is phenomenal—and the broth is what makes a truly fine soup. We'll be back for more.

We thought the chicken chow mein ($6.95) was a little greasy, but sometimes a little grease is good: we scarfed the whole dish.

Lemongrass is thriftiest at lunch, when it runs $5.25 to $6.25 per plate, with rice. Lemongrass regulars Eddie and Mary like to grab a couple of Kung Pao Chicken plates to eat later at Punalu'u Black Sand beach, a little over an hour's drive away, or dine in on a Saturday night. Sounds like a plan!

CUISINE   **Deli/pizzeria with fresh locally grown fruit**

LOCATION   **Mauka side of Main Street**

HOURS   **Monday-Thursday, 8 a.m. to 7 p.m.; Friday and Saturday, 8 a.m. to 8 p.m.; Sunday, 8 a.m. to 6 p.m.**

SEATING   **25, indoors and out**

PARKING   **In front and along sides of building**

OPENED   **1920; current owners have had it since 2001**

ALCOHOL   **No**

PLASTIC   **MC, V, JCB**

NOTES   **The owners grow all the fruit and produce sold in the store and use many organic ingredients.**

Naalehu Fruit Stand
Main Street, Nāʻālehu
Telephone 929-9009

Naalehu Fruit Stand transcends its simple name. This little gem in the middle of beautifully bucolic Nāʻālehu town serves up some of the best sandwiches, coffee, baked goods and pizza on the island, with plenty of aloha. Whether you're headed out to the green and black sand beaches of the Kaʻu District or just passing through, consider lunch here. Their pizza is one of my favorites on the island, built from scratch with organic whole-wheat flour pastry dough and a zesty tomato sauce with organic spices ($8 for a 12-inch pie, $1 for each topping). *Mama mia!* Other items, like the BBQ Tofu Sandwich ($3.25), the Manapua ($1.05 each) and the

Chef Salad ($3.25), get rave reviews. It's a great little menu, with very thrifty pricing.

For a real treat, sink your sweet tooth into the sticky Macadamia Nut Shortbread, baked by owner Lea Koomoa-Gulpaʻn. She and her husband Roland live the good life, creating delicious, inexpensive and healthy food and raising their family in the paradise of Nāʻālehu. When he's not out fishing for the daily catch special, or plucking fruit from their farm, Roland is behind the counter, cheerfully ringing up orders with pure aloha spirit. You can feel and taste the happiness.

CUISINE	**Sandwiches, plate lunches and bakery items**
LOCATION	**Highway 11 in Nāʻālehu**
WEB	**www.punaluubakeshop.com**
HOURS	**Daily, 9 a.m. to 5 p.m.**
SEATING	**80**
PARKING	**Plenty**
OPENED	**1991**
ALCOHOL	**No**
PLASTIC	**A, D, JCB, MC, V**

Punalu'u Bake Shop & Gift Shop
95-5642 Māmalahoa Highway, Nā'ālehu
Telephone 929-7343

This spotless and charming roadside attraction is a must-stop for anyone traveling around the island or heading to the nearby black sand beach, and it's a worthwhile destination for a Sunday drive. Its claim to fame is that it's the southernmost bakery in the nation, but Punalu'u Bake Shop is much more than a geographical point, and more than a bakery.

For instance, the Roast Pork with Gravy Plate Lunch ($6.95) is as moist and succulent as you'd hope, even without the gravy. It's so large you might need a nap after consuming it, even without the potato-macaroni salad and rice that come with all their plate lunches. The bakery's signature soft-textured Punalu'u Sweet Bread is baked fresh daily and is the star of the sandwich menu, showing up in such delights as the tasty Seafood Supreme sandwich ($4.99), which contains a seafood salad of shrimp, imitation crab meat and mayonnaise. The 24-ounce loaves are available in several flavors (guava, taro, coconut, cinnamon-raisin and macadamia nut) and make welcome gifts. You can watch the bakery crew at work through the exhibition windows, which reveal a gleaming kitchen.

Punalu'u Bake Shop offers picturesque seating in gazebos nestled alongside a gurgling waterfall, amid resplendent tropical landscaping. The newly renovated gift shop features an array of island-inspired trinkets, artwork and food items, but most irresistible is the new bakery display case, which shamelessly tempts customers with homemade malasadas, cookies, macadamia nut cinnamon rolls (we consumed one of these in less than two minutes), pies and more. Save some calories for the Punalu'u Bake Shop—it's well worth the drive.

CUISINE	**Authentic Mexican**
LOCATION	**Catty-corner to Black Rock Cafe**
HOURS	**Daily, 7 a.m. to 9 p.m.; breakfast: 7 a.m. to 11 a.m.; lunch/dinner: 11 a.m. to 9 p.m.**
SEATING	**122 in the restaurant; 98 in the bar**
PARKING	**Free parking lot nearby; parking along Main Street**
OPENED	**1986**
ALCOHOL	**Full bar. Try the Lilikoi margarita with li hing mui salt around the rim.**
PLASTIC	**All cards**
NOTE	**Owner Sal Luquin raises and slaughters his own beef and pork for the restaurant.**

Luquin's Mexican Restaurant
15-2942 Pāhoa Government Road, Pāhoa
Telephone 965-9990

Luquin's is a wonderful place to take the family, especially if your family is rowdy like ours and loves to have a good time slurping margaritas and filling up on Mexican food.

My mother-out-law and I always start with a signature Cuervo Gold Lilikoi (passionfruit) margarita, dusted with ling hing mui powder ($6). Salut! It goes down fast, and that ice-freeze headache is a mean one. A few tortilla chips dunked in home-made spicy hot salsa will melt the freeze. The first basket is free; the second one is $2.50.

I always faithfully order the *muy excellente* Carnitas dinner platter: chopped fried pork that Sal Luquin raises and slaughters himself, that wild *caballero*. It's served with corn tortillas, plus *muy bueno* rice and beans, for $11. I spoon on the salsa and savor every bite. I never have room for dessert, but I'll take another Lilikoi 'rita, *por favor*.

Steve and his brother go for the Chile Relleno Dinner, a large green pepper stuffed with cheese and served with rice and beans ($7.25) and we all usually share a Cheese Quesadilla or two ($4.75). Mother-out-law likes the Flauta, beef rolled up in a flour tortilla and deep-fried. It's served with sour cream and, when the avocadoes are in season, gua-camole, for $5.25. We always leave way too full but look forward to coming back.

Vayamos, amigos!

CUISINE	**Homestyle American cooking with a little local flair**
LOCATION	**Nā'ālehu's Main Street, on the makai side**
HOURS	**Daily, breakfast: 10 a.m. to 2 p.m.; lunch: 10 a.m. to 5 p.m.; dinner: 5 p.m. to 9 p.m.**
SEATING	**About 50 in the restaurant and in the covered outdoor area combined; about 25 in the lounge**
PARKING	**Plenty of free parking in the front**
OPENED	**1998**
ALCOHOL	**Full bar**
PLASTIC	**MC, V**
NOTES	**This is the southernmost bar and restaurant in the United States.**

22

Shaka Restaurant
95-5673 Old Māmalahoa Highway, Nāʻālehu
Telephone 929-7404

My favorite thrifty restaurants are those that go the extra mile and make their own sauces, dressings and gravies in addition to everything else on the menu. After tasting owner Shirley Bolton's homemade tartar sauce, I was hooked.

My server suggested the Fresh Fish Sandwich, featuring whatever Island fish is biting for the South Point fishermen. The day I went in, it was mahimahi, served grilled on a sesame-seed bun with lettuce, pickles, red onion, a side of fries and, best of all, the homemade tartar sauce, $8.95. My, oh, my! After swallowing the sandwich hook, line and sinker, I just had to try a piece of the Honey-Dipped Fried Chicken ($7.50 for two pieces, served with all the trimmings). We're talking golden-brown, crispy chicken worth clucking about.

I also tasted a spoonful of Shirley's homemade blue cheese dressing, which is worth the 75 cents for a side order. Wow! Her homemade biscuits are to die for, too. And for the keiki, a wonderfully thrifty, kid-centric menu of hot dogs and fries ($3), mac & cheese ($2.50), and shrimp & fries ($4) will keep them happy.

The Hawaiian "shaka" sign (pinkie and thumb outstretched, other digits bent against the palm) means "hang loose." Go hang loose and get some tasty, thrifty grinds at the southernmost restaurant in the U.S.

CUISINE	**Regional Thai (featuring fresh Big Island ingredients)**
LOCATION	**Volcano Village**
HOURS	**Nightly, 5 p.m. to 9 p.m.; last seating at 8:30 p.m. sharp; from 8:30 p.m., take-out /outside seating available**
SEATING	**45**
PARKING	**Parking lot**
OPENED	**1999**
ALCOHOL	**Full bar, Thai beer**
PLASTIC	**V, MC, A, JCB, D**
NOTES	**Reservations are recommended.**

23

Thai Thai Restaurant
19-8048 Old Volcano Road, Volcano Village
Telephone 967-7969

A visit to the fiery, feisty volcano goddess Pele requires fiery, feisty food—a little taste of what's to come, perhaps. Lucky for us, the flavors explode at Thai Thai Restaurant, located in little Volcano Village, a lava stone's throw from the entrance to Hawai'i Volcanoes National Park.

The fresh Thai cuisine erupts with savory appeal, thanks to the skills of chef/owner Jiranan Thomas and to the farmers of the wet, tropical East Hawai'i region who grow all the wonderful produce that comprises Thai food: green papaya, chili pepper, cilantro, kaffir lime leaves, ginger, basil, lemongrass and more.

Thai Thai isn't as inexpensive as locals would like, but choose carefully and one person can eat and tip with a $20 bill—just skip that alcohol. On my next trip, I'll consider the Chicken Satay appetizer as an entrée. It's delicious and filling (order a side of jasmine rice, $1.29), plus it's entrée-priced at $15.99. Best of all, it's served with Jiranan's peanut sauce, which is the best I've had: dark, woody brown and viscous, not the runny peanut butter-based sauces that dampen my appetite.

Many entrées run $8.99 to $10.99, like the popular chicken panang curry with red chili peppers, coconut milk and seasonal veggies. A word to the wise: unless you want your throat to burn like molten lava, order Medium. Hot and Thai Hot are for Thai tastebuds only, or utter masochists. With Medium, I broke a sweat and got that welcome *zap*! I love. Put out the fire with imported Thai jackfruit ice cream ($2.99).

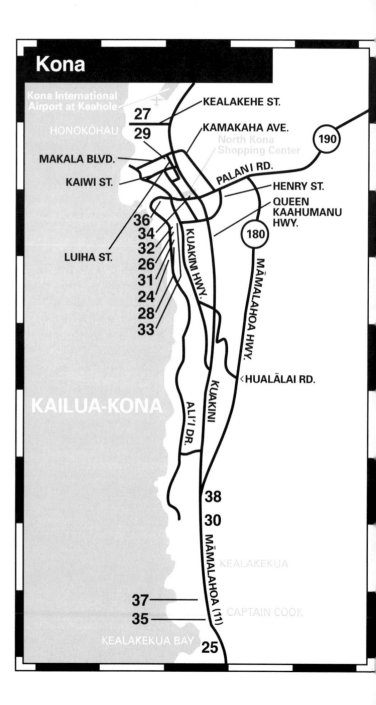

Kona

Kona International Airport at Keahole

KEALAKEHE ST.

27
29

HONOKŌHAU

KAMAKAHA AVE.

North Kona Shopping Center

190

MAKALA BLVD.

KAIWI ST.

PALANI RD.

HENRY ST.

QUEEN KAAHUMANU HWY.

36
34
32
26
31
24
28
33

LUIHA ST.

KUAKINI HWY.

180

MĀMALAHOA HWY.

KAILUA-KONA

ALI'I DR.

KUAKINI

‹HUALĀLAI RD.

38

30

MĀMALAHOA

KEALAKEKUA

37

35

MĀMALAHOA (11)

CAPTAIN COOK

KEALAKEKUA BAY

25

Kona

Breakfast

Lunch

Dinner

CUISINE	**Southern-style American**
LOCATION	**Oceanfront on Waterfront Row, across from the Farmer's Market**
WEB	**www.bubbagump.com**
HOURS	**Breakfast daily, 7 a.m. to 10:30 a.m.; lunch/dinner, 11 a.m. to 10 p.m. Sunday-Thursday (bar/pupus available until 11 p.m.); 11 a.m. to 11 p.m. Friday and Saturday (bar/pupus available until midnight)**
SEATING	**272**
PARKING	**Pay parking underneath Waterfront Row; limited parking along Ali'i Drive**
OPENED	**1999**
ALCOHOL	**Full bar**
PLASTIC	**All cards**
NOTES	**This is currently the only Bubba Gump in the chain serving breakfast.**

Bubba Gump
75-5776 Ali'i Drive, Kailua-Kona
Telephone 331-8442

My friend Andrea has lived in Kona for 23 years and knows where to eat. But I was skeptical when she suggested Bubba Gump for breakfast. What would a Hollywood-inspired shrimp-shack chain possibly know about the day's first meal?

A lot, it turns out. We sipped yummy vanilla lattes ($3) on the oceanfront deck and pondered Mama's Special Pancake Plate with homemade vanilla bean syrup and fresh berries ($6.99); the three-egg Cajun Omelet with pepper-jack cheese, andouille sausage, onions, peppers and tomatoes with potatoes and toast for $8.29; and the Steak & Eggs for $10.99. We couldn't decide, so we ordered all three in the name of research.

While we waited, I couldn't keep my eyes off the spectacular ocean scenery. Bubba Gump is located right on the waterfront, so close you could get splashed by a big south swell. Anchored offshore were the new *Pride of Aloha* cruise ship and several small sailboats. I envied the dozens of triathlete swimmers slicing through Kailua Bay—that is, until breakfast arrived.

We dove into the pancakes, the omelet and the steak and eggs—a gluttonous triathlon in itself. The pancakes were fabulous, perfected by the vanilla bean syrup; the fluffy omelet had a wonderful kick with the spicy andouille sausage and pepper jack; and the steak and eggs were cooked to perfection. It was flawless.

There are also daily specials for $6.29, a great kid's menu and a Bubba Gump retail shop. Stop, Forrest, Stop!

CUISINE	**Homestyle bakery and deli, with a local flair**
LOCATION	**Between mile markers 108 and 109 on the makai (ocean) side**
WEB	**www.coffeeshack.com**
HOURS	**Daily, 7 a.m. to 4 p.m.**
SEATING	**50**
PARKING	**Limited parking lot—try across and along the highway if it's full**
OPENED	**1995**
ALCOHOL	**Wine and beer, tropical mimosas**
PLASTIC	**MC, V, D**
NOTES	**Check out the quaint gift shop for a perfect souvenir.**

25

The Coffee Shack
83-5799 Māmalahoa Highway (Highway 19), Captain Cook
Telephone 328-9555

The first thing that will capture your attention when you walk into The Coffee Shack is the priceless view. Perched high above Kealakekua Bay on a sheer cliff, you can observe the very bay Captain James Cook sailed into, changing Hawai'i forever. On a clear day, you can see all the way to Ka La'e, or South Point, the first place the ancient Polynesians landed their ocean-going canoes—changing Hawai'i forever. It's a powerful view—drink it in.

The second thing to capture your attention will be this fabulous little eatery's aromas and menu. Just about everything here is homemade and amazing, from the breads, pastries and desserts to the homegrown 100-percent pure Kona coffee ($1.50 for a bottomless cup). I like to fuel a day's adventures with the smooth java and their Eggs Benedict: two fresh Holualoa eggs on top of toasted home baked English muffins and Canadian bacon, slathered in house-made hollandaise with just a hint of nutmeg, $8.95. Hallelujah! It's the most perfect Eggs Benedict I've tasted in Hawai'i.

Homemade breakfast pastries like scones, banana bread and cinnamon rolls range from $2.50 to $3, and there's irresistible French Toast with Homemade Luau Bread featuring locally grown macadamia nuts, pineapple chunks, coconut and carrots, all topped with powdered sugar, for $7.50. Yowza! All the breads and desserts are homemade, and lunch is terrific, too.

Stop by and gulp down the view and the food. You'll be pleasantly surprised.

CUISINE	**Casual café**
LOCATION	**Kona Marketplace, across from Huliheʻe Palace**
WEB	**www.hulabean.com**
HOURS	**Daily, 7:30 a.m. to 9:30 p.m.**
SEATING	**18**
PARKING	**Public parking on ground floor of the condominium behind the restaurant; limited parking along Aliʻi Drive**
OPENED	**October 2000**
ALCOHOL	**No**
PLASTIC	**All cards**
NOTES	**Make time to visit Huliheʻe Palace across the street, now a museum full of beautiful furniture and fascinating Hawaiian artifacts.**

26

Hula Bean
75-5719 Ali'i Drive, #E, Kailua-Kona
Telephone 329-6152

If you want to explore Kailua-Kona by foot, the best time to go is early in the morning before the sun gets too high in the sky. It's inspiring to see the swimmers hit the water near Kailua Pier and stroke their way across the bay. You can watch them as you walk down Ali'i Drive on your way to the cute little Hula Bean café for breakfast and a terrific cup of 100-percent top-of-the-line Kona coffee.

I doubt that there's a cheaper, better breakfast in Kona. At Hula Bean, you can get a bagel and cream cheese for a mere $2, two scrambled eggs and toast for $3, or a Breakfast Sandwich served on a croissant with ham, egg and cheese for only $4.25.

Or you can be naughty like me and have a 16-ounce Chocolate Decadence Big Island Ice Cream milk shake for $4.95 and call it a calcium-rich smoothie. But what is truly amazing is the coffee.

You can buy six grades of world-famous Kona coffee here. Hula Bean sells only the finest, 100-percent state-certified, extra-fancy-grade Kona coffee, which represents the top of the bean heap. The beans' consistent size ensures even roasting and a premium flavor. The coffee goes for $1.58 for an 8-ounce cup, or $24.95 for a whole pound of dark-roast beans. This is seriously great java. Stop by, have breakfast and savor the flavor.

CUISINE	**American with an emphasis on fresh fish**
LOCATION	**At the Honokōhau Small Boat Harbor**
HOURS	**Monday-Saturday, 11 a.m. to 7 p.m.; Sunday, 11 a.m. to 5:30 p.m.**
SEATING	**Around 150**
PARKING	**Free parking lot at the harbor**
OPENED	**1990, under new ownership since 2000**
ALCOHOL	**Full bar**
PLASTIC	**A, JCB, MC, V**
NOTES	**Fresh fish is the specialty.**

27

Harbor House
74-425 Kealakehe Parkway, Honokōhau
Telephone 326-4166

My friends and I come to Harbor House for three reasons: the ice-cold schooners of Steinlager, the fresh-off-the-boat fish sandwiches and the location.

Harbor House is located three miles north of Kona at Honokōhau Harbor, headquarters for the rollicking sportfishing fleet that transports the masses out to the deep, marlin-rich waters off the Kona Coast. It's perched above the marina, and attracts a mixture of tourists, fishing boat guys, salty sea gals, and sailors quenching their thirst after a long day (or month) on the ocean.

Do we care that the sexy female bartenders would rather entertain the regulars surrounding them at the bar than give us a second glance? Or that the regulars eye every female who walks in like she was the catch of the day? Nah, because being in Harbor House on a Friday afternoon is like walking into a Jimmy Buffett song at full volume.

We like to sit at a harbor-front table, throw back a few 18-ounce schooners ($3 regular, $2.75 at happy hour) and watch the action on the docks below. We munch fresh fish sandwiches for $8.50, served with plank fries. I like the fresh ono, a firm, thick filet called wahoo in other zip codes. If payday is long gone, then it's fries and beer only.

Head to the end of the harbor and enjoy the gorgeous Kona sunset at the little beach past the fuel dock. And don't let the bartenders scare you—they warm up with bright smiles eventually.

CUISINE	**Fresh kava drinks & Hawaiian food**
LOCATION	**Coconut Grove Marketplace**
WEB	**www.kanakakava.com**
HOURS	**Sunday-Wednesday, 11 a.m. to 10 p.m.; Thursday-Saturday, 11 a.m. to 11 p.m.**
SEATING	**Limited: Three at the bar, eight at the two small tables and benches on the lanai. Many customers stand around and socialize.**
PARKING	**Ample free parking at Coconut Grove Marketplace**
OPENED	**September 2001**
ALCOHOL	**None, but they specialize in the mildly intoxicating kava**
PLASTIC	**Cash only**
NOTES	**There is also an oxygen bar for all you airheads.**

28

Kanaka Kava, Hawaiian Awa Bar & Restaurant
75-5803 Ali'i Dr., Kailua-Kona
Telephone 327-1660

If you're looking for an authentic Hawaiian experience, head to Kanaka Kava. You'll get a history lesson with every sip of the namesake kava beverage and every bite of Hawaiian food.

The ancient Melanesians discovered that the mildly narcotic root of the native kava, or 'awa, plant produced a relaxing buzz, and its use spread throughout Polynesia. Kava sailed to Hawai'i with the early Polynesian settlers, and has since become an integral part of cultural ceremonies, including chiefly encounters, canoe blessings and so on.

The owners of Kanaka Kava grow organic kava on their Puuala Farm & Ranch in Hamakua and serve it in a traditional coconut shell ($3). You can drink it straight or with juice ($4), which helps mask the earthy flavor. Chug it, and you'll likely enjoy an instant relaxation and a slight tingling numbness in the mouth and lips. Kava will not impair your vision or your mind.

To maximize its effects, kava should be enjoyed on an empty stomach. But maybe you prefer a Hawaiian meal to a native buzz. The tender Kalua Pork ($4 a la carte) is baked in a traditional *imu*, or underground oven, and is the best I've had. Kanaka Kava is one of but a handful of restaurants to offer *'ulu*, or breadfruit, a Polynesian staple starch. Get it steamed in coconut milk, $4. Heavenly! There is opihi, a native shellfish, served raw or cooked for $4, and other traditional items very hard to find in restaurants. *I mua!* (We go!)

CUISINE **Mexican American**

LOCATION **The Old Industrial Area, near the corner of Kaiwi and Luhia streets**

HOURS **Closed Sundays**

SEATING **25**

PARKING **Ample parking in the parking lot out front and along Luhia Street**

OPENED **2000**

ALCOHOL **BYO beer/wine only**

PLASTIC **Cash only**

NOTES **Also check out Killer Tacos in Hale'iwa, Oahu.**

29

Killer Tacos
74-5483 Kaiwi Street, Kailua-Kona
Telephone 329-3335

I love a place where you can pick up a tasty, healthy bite in the $5 range, and that's what you'll find in Kona's Old Industrial area at Killer Tacos.

Surfers, locals and people who work in the area frequent Killer Tacos, and business has been booming since they opened their doors in 2000. Surf videos play continuously on a big TV, and the mood is casual and fun.

Nine times out of 10, I'll order the Shortboard Burrito, a flour tortilla chock-full of rice, black beans (or refried pintos), cheese, fresh salsa and chicken (you can also choose spicy ground beef or kalua pig), for a mere $3.99. If your appetite is bottomless, bite the big one (as in dollar) and get the Longboard Burrito, a heavy-duty monster stuffed with all the Shortboard ingredients, plus sour cream and guacamole, for a buck more.

Every once in a while I'll get unpredictable and order the Super Nachos ($4.99), which are some of the cheapest, best nachos around. They're served in a big basket with melted cheese, salsa, sour cream, guacamole, and your choice of meat. The most expensive item on the menu is the Killer Taco Salad at $5.99, and the prices are the same for lunch or dinner. An unbeatable deal.

CUISINE	**Healthy gourmet**
LOCATION	**North Kealakekua on the mauka side of the "highway," between mile markers 112 & 113**
HOURS	**Monday-Friday, 8 a.m. to 5 p.m.; closed weekends**
SEATING	**86**
PARKING	**Ample parking in front**
OPENED	**October 2001**
ALCOHOL	**BYOB; $10 corkage fee for wine**
PLASTIC	**MC, V, JCB**
NOTES	**Now serving breakfast.**

30

Nasturtium Café
79-7491 Māmalahoa Highway, Kealakekua
Telephone 322-5083

I adore every aspect of Nasturtium Café: the healthy menu, the design, the location, and the philosophy of chef/owner Diane, whose goal is to feed the mind, body and spirit of every guest with healthy, tasty food that nourishes the physical body and stimulates the senses.

Diane has feng-shui'd what used to be a 1920s auto garage into a beautiful roadside sanctuary with a flourishing garden, a riot of edible nasturtium flowers, and outrageously creative food that addresses a variety of needs. Diabetics, people with wheat allergies, the lactose-intolerant, those on low-fat, blood-type or Atkins diets, whoever—all are easily accommodated at Nasturtium Café. I arrive craving light, healthy fuel.

As I sip her divine rosehip hibiscus lemonade ($3), Diane presents a mammoth green salad, a cup of Mexican corn soup, and fresh-baked bread. The greens are grown by local farmers and tossed with red onion, cherry tomatoes, herbs and orange nasturtium flowers, dressed with olive oil and balsamic vinegar dressing. The soup is delicious, thick without being rich, non-dairy and made from scratch with sweet corn. Jalapeños lend a potent kick. This salad/soup combo goes for $6.95 with a cup of the soup, $8.95 with a bowl. There are three soups a day to choose from.

But the menu goes so far beyond soup and salad I vow to return. You'll find lean meats like ostrich and bison as well as several innovative, guilt-free desserts (see Sweet Endings). It's no wonder the Food Network featured Nasturtium Café on a recent show.

CUISINE	Take-out sushi
LOCATION	Kona Marketplace (across the street from the Historic Kona Inn Shopping Center)—not to be confused with Coconut Grove Marketplace)
HOURS	Monday-Friday, 10:30a.m. to 7 p.m.; Saturday, 11 a.m. to 7 p.m.; closed Sunday.
SEATING	12 or so; most people get take-out
PARKING	Ample, both free and paid
OPENED	June 2000
ALCOHOL	No
PLASTIC	V, MC
NOTES	They also create very affordable party platters ranging from $23 to $40.

31

You Make the Roll
75-5725 Ali'i Dr., #D-101, Kailua-Kona
Telephone 326-1322

You Make the Roll is not do-it-yourself sushi, as the name might lead you to expect; it's really a "have it your way" grab-and-go sushi restaurant with very friendly prices.

You choose from 21 different ingredients; they roll your choices into tasty maki sushi rolls or nigiri sushi pieces. My "signature" roll is crab, avocado and daikon pickle. Go wild and roll up four, five or six different ingredients for $3.99, $4.99 and $5.99 respectively.

If you're not feeling creative, You Make the Roll has a menu of sushi favorites ranging from the ubiquitous (the California roll) to the outrageous (the Hurricane roll: teriyaki chicken, crab, avocado, tomato and green onion topped with melted cheese).

I managed to feed myself, four rather large guys and a girlfriend for less then $50 (including tip and tax). Not only that—there was so much left over that one lucky fellow got to take home a doggie bag. We tried 15 different rolls: Tempura Shrimp, Big Island, Spicy Tuna, Teri Chicken, a couple of kamikaze rolls we designed ourselves and the daily special. That's only $3 a roll! A total steal.

An important thing to know about You Make the Roll is that there are a few tables, but the sushi is served in plastic, ready to go—perfect fuel for a day of exploring the Big Island, and an easy solution for a potluck party.

CUISINE	**Fresh local-style**
LOCATION	**Near the DMV**
HOURS	**Daily, breakfast, 6 a.m. to 10 a.m.; lunch, 11 a.m. to 2 p.m.; dinner, 5 p.m. to 9 p.m.**
SEATING	**80**
PARKING	**Daytime parking a challenge in the crowded lot; evening not as bad**
OPENED	**December 2002**
ALCOHOL	**BYOB**
PLASTIC	**D, MC, V**

32

Big Island Grill
75-5702 Kuakini Highway, Kailua-Kona
Telephone 326-1153

I love "yin and yang" meals: something delicious but fattening (coconut-fried shrimp) disguised as something healthy (a salad). You don't feel guilty, because it's a salad, but you're not entirely deprived because there's fried stuff. I'd heard about the Coconut Shrimp Salad at the Big Island Grill and decided to pay homage.

By some miracle, five of us managed to find a table during the dinner rush. We shared a family-style feast of Roast Pork ($6.75), a massive slab of Baby-Back Ribs ($16), a Seafood Stir-Fry ($14), and the aforementioned yin and yang salad ($11.75). Not one complaint.

While the menu is locally inspired, this is no standard plate lunch joint. Dressings and sauces, like the plum chili sauce and the creamy sesame dressing drizzled over the Coconut Shrimp Salad, are homemade. The roast pork, which elsewhere can be bland, is flavorful here, encrusted with Hawaiian rock salt, cracked pepper and fresh rosemary, topped with luscious gravy that does not come from a can. Most desserts (there are 10) are also homemade. (See Sweet Endings.)

In charge of the stoves is owner Bruce Goold, once a chef at the old Regency Hotel and the King Kamehameha Beach Hotel. (His wife Maile, their children, and extended family members help run the place.) Someone in charge who has cooking skills and restaurant experience? What a concept! It sure works for Big Island Grill.

CUISINE   **Casual Japanese and sake**

LOCATION **Below the Kona Plaza condominiums**

HOURS   **Nightly, 5 p.m. to 11 p.m.**

SEATING   **32 inside, 28 outside, 10 at sushi bar**

PARKING   **Limited along Ali'i Drive; some free parking in the condos' parking lot**

OPENED   **September 2003**

ALCOHOL   **Full bar, with a superior sake collection; the only Big Island restaurant to feature Kirin Ichiban on draft**

PLASTIC   **All cards**

NOTES   **Come early for happy hour (5 p.m. to 6 p.m.)—draft beers are only a buck.**

33

Izakaya Kai
75-5719 Ali'i Drive, Kailua-Kona
Telephone 329-2002

When you finally find Izakaya Kai in the labyrinth of downtown Kona, the servers and manager greet you with a boisterous *"Irashaimase!"* (Welcome to the restaurant!) And so the fun begins.

An *izakaya* is a casual Japanese pub where friends go to drink and share appetizers, a concept my ambassador to Kona, Andrea, knew would appeal to me. *Kai* means "oar" in Japanese and "ocean" in Hawaiian.

Andrea is such a regular that our server knew exactly what we'd eat: Yakibifun, a light stir-fried noodle dish with shrimp and veggies, $7, and the Saikoro Steak, seasoned and sautéed to perfection, $8.50, served with a salad in sesame-ginger dressing. While these are appetizers, they're big enough to be entrées, and they are scrumptious. We

had to try the homemade pork and beef dumplings, or Gyoza, for a mere $6; the Spicy Tuna Sushi Roll, only $4.50 for six pieces; a huge, fresh Daikon Salad, $4.50 (with the same sesame-ginger dressing); and the foil-baked Portabella Mushroom Special, $5. The food was so *oishi* (delicious) and so inexpensive we ordered way too much, finally ending with Andrea's favorite, a delectable Tempura-Fried Green Tea Ice Cream, $4.50.

While the sake and the draft Kirin Ichiban are popular, I love the Vodka and Grapefruit cocktail. Two halves of a ruby red grapefruit are juiced tableside, then poured over a generous glass of vodka and ice. At $6.50 it's not cheap, but it's a good pour and extraordinarily tasty.

Irashaimase, indeed!

CUISINE	**Pizza, salads, sandwiches**
LOCATION	**Tucked behind the Firestone station on the corner of Kuakini Highway and Palani Road**
WEB	**www.KonaBrewingCo.com**
HOURS	**Sunday-Thursday, 11 a.m. to 9 p.m.; Friday and Saturday, 11 a.m. to 10 p.m.**
SEATING	**174**
PARKING	**Limited parking outside pub**
OPENED	**1994**
ALCOHOL	**Delicious hand-crafted lagers and ales; full bar**
PLASTIC	**D, MC, V**

34

Kona Brewing Company
75-5629 Kuakini Highway, Kailua-Kona
Telephone 334-BREW (2739)

This local favorite almost didn't make the list—my bills there have been less-than-thrifty due to the amount of terrific Kona Brewing Company lager my friends and I are capable of quaffing. But if you leave alcohol out of the equation, Kona Brewing Company serves up great food for an affordable price.

Take the Roasted Garlic pupu at $5.99. A gigantic head of garlic is oven-roasted to a perfect golden brown and served with toasted focaccia. Spread the soft cloves on the bread, dip into the warm Gorgonzola cheese that comes with it, and heaven! Pair this with a Big Island Side Salad ($5.49), and you have a satisfying meal. On my last excursion, my friends and I shared appetizers and small pizzas and left content. I nearly spewed beer laughing as my friend Laurel pulled the thriftiest move I've ever seen and concocted her own lemonade: she ordered ice water with lots of lemon wedges and stirred in a pack of Equal.

The pizza here is some of the best on the island ($20.99 for my favorite, the 14-inch Kona Wild Mushroom, with an olive oil base, mozzarella, goat cheese, wild mushrooms, roasted garlic, onions and red peppers, oh my!); and the Strawberry Spinach Salad, with fresh strawberries, macadamia nuts, Gorgonzola and Maui onions ($7.99), is also quite good. I hear the sandwiches are superb, and are served on "Fire Rock Spelt Grain Focaccia Rolls." I'll save that for the next edition.

CUISINE **Homestyle American, with a little local flair**

LOCATION **Captain Cook on the makai side of the road**

HOURS **Tuesday-Sunday, breakfast: 7 a.m. to 9 a.m.; lunch: 11 a.m. to 2 p.m.; dinner: 5 p.m. to 7:30 p.m.**

SEATING **62**

PARKING **The Manago Hotel has 2 parking lots, and there are public stalls in front**

OPENED **1917**

ALCOHOL **Beer, wine and standard bar liquor**

PLASTIC **Everything but A**

NOTES **Room rates at this historic landmark hotel are ultra thrifty, ranging from $49 to $54 per night.**

35

Manago Hotel Restaurant
82-6155 Māmalahoa Hwy., Captain Cook
Telephone 323-2642

Manago's first claim to fame is that it's an integral part of Big Island history. Owner Dwight Manago's grandparents opened the hotel 87 years ago, and it served as temporary home base for the migrant workers plying the fertile agricultural region of South Kona.

Manago's second claim to fame is the restaurant's pork chops. I had friends threaten to boycott this book unless I wrote about Manago's pork chops. This was a dilemma for me—my favorite movie is *Babe*, and I'm not hog-wild about *the other white meat*. But Manago's regulars are—the restaurant cooks up 1,500 pounds of Big Island pork every month.

I drove an hour just to taste what the fuss what about, and ordered the combo: one pork chop and one fresh ono filet ($8.75), thinking I'd take a gratuitous bite out of the chop and focus on the fish. Fish, schmish. One bite of that crispy, thin, "just like Mom used to make" pan-fried chop, and I was in hog heaven. There I was, gnawing the meat off the bone like some depraved carnivore.

All entrees come with three side dishes plus a jumbo bowl of sticky white rice. Good thing my friend Suzy was with me. We got lima beans, canned corn with peas and bacon, and a terrific potato-macaroni salad, served family-style.

I'll definitely be back to pig out on Manago's pork chops again, because this little piggy went *whee whee whee*! all the way home.

CUISINE	**American/seafood**
LOCATION	**Across from the King Kamehameha Hotel**
HOURS	**Daily, lunch: 11 a.m. to 5 p.m.; dinner: 5 p.m. to 11 p.m.; bar open 11 a.m. to 11 p.m.**
SEATING	**Around 115**
PARKING	**Some stalls out front, public pay-parking at the King Kamehameha Hotel**
OPENED	**January 1979**
ALCOHOL	**Full bar**
PLASTIC	**MC, V**

36

Quinn's Almost By The Sea
75-5655-A Palani Road, Kailua-Kona
Telephone 329-3822

I first started going to Quinn's a decade ago, and I'm happy to report it's still Kailua town's best place to get a great meal at an affordable price. Located at the start of Ali'i Drive just past the Kuakini Highway intersection, Quinn's is a beloved Kailua landmark.

What I like best about Quinn's, in addition to the delicious American-style cuisine, are the prices and the ambience. The covered outdoor lanai has just enough romance and just enough beach-town casual to make it appealing for everyone. I go with my friend Andrea and her family, who know the menu inside and out.

"Get the Steak Sandwich without the bun," advises Andrea. I see why—what arrives is a 5-ounce filet mignon served with salad for a mere $10.95. Given the price of beef, try making filet and salad at home for less than that. Her mom has the popular Fish and Chips ($9.95), made with fresh mahimahi fried in Quinn's batter, with homemade tartar sauce and fries. I grab a few bites: the fish is thick, white, very fresh and, despite the fried batter treatment, not at all greasy.

Everything is wonderful at Quinn's—the salad dressings are homemade; the wine is never more than $4 a glass; the service is always friendly, informative and prompt. It's no wonder everyone keeps going back.

CUISINE	**Mexican**
LOCATION	**Across the street from the Captain Cook Fire Station**
HOURS	**Daily, 11 a.m. to 9 p.m.**
SEATING	**75, indoors and outdoors**
PARKING	**Parking stalls adjacent to restaurant**
OPENED	**1996; under new ownership since June 2003**
ALCOHOL	**Excellent margaritas, beer, wine**
PLASTIC	**A, MC, V, DC, JCB**
NOTES	**Ask about the unprinted but reasonably priced children's menu.**

37

Señor Billy's Cantina
82-6023 Māmalahoa Highway, Captain Cook
Telephone 323-2012

aptain Cook is an hour's drive from the Kohala Coast, but that doesn't stop me from going there after work for the great Mexican food and margaritas at Señor Billy's. My best friend Suzy lives about a block away from the restaurant, and we love to make it a girl's night out with a few margaritas and some homemade south-of-the-border grinds.

We always start with a decidedly unthrifty Silver Coin margarita (mine frozen, hers on the rocks, salt on both, please), with Herradura Silver agave tequila and Cointreau, $7. If it's payday, we have two; if not, it's time to order our favorite: the Fajitas, a signature dish of flame-grilled marinated steak or chicken (we like steak), roasted veggies, guacamole, sour cream, house-made fire-roasted salsa and warm flour tortillas. In my opinion, these are the best fajitas on the island. They're $11.99, so we split them and then "fill in the blanks" with a less-expensive appetizer (like my favorite, the Double Stuffed BBQ Duck Quesadilla, $8.99) or sometimes just the complimentary chips and salsa.

One word describes Señor Billy's house-made fire-roasted salsa, with its sultry hint of smoky chipotle: incredible! Other outrageously delish items include the Mexican rice and the pinto and black beans. Beans and rice might be the nuts and bolts of Mexican cuisine, but they're also the true test of a great Mexican joint, and Señor Billy's definitely makes the grade.

CUISINE	**Local-style Japanese**
LOCATION	**Next to the Shell gas station**
HOURS	**Daily, breakfast: 6:30 a.m. to 11 a.m.; lunch: 11 a.m. to 1:45 p.m.; dinner: 5 p.m. to 9 p.m.**
SEATING	**Main dining room: 80**
PARKING	**Ample parking in lot**
OPENED	**First opened in 1929 as a general merchandise store; opened as a restaurant in the 1940s after World War II began**
ALCOHOL	**Full bar**
PLASTIC	**Cash and travelers' checks only; ATM onsite**
NOTES	**Private functions are often held in the upstairs banquet room; there's seating for 100 there.**

38

Teshima's Restaurant
79-7251 Māmalahoa Highway, Kealakekua
Telephone 322-9140

No Big Island food book would be worth its salt if it didn't pay homage to Teshima's Restaurant. Teshima's is a Kealakekua landmark and has been enormously popular with locals since it opened in the 1940s.

Owner Shizuko Teshima is 97 years old. She originally opened Teshima's in 1929 as a general store and then turned it into a Japanese restaurant right after World War II broke out, and she still works tirelessly to keep her pride and joy the success story it is today. If you're lucky, she'll stop by your table and share some of her fascinating life stories with you.

While the Teshima Omelet Fried Rice ($8.75) with beef, chicken or Portuguese sausage is the perennial local favorite, my personal favorite is the No. 3 Teishoku, a Japanese dinner that comes complete with miso soup, fresh sashimi, beef sukiyaki (cooked with shoyu), shrimp tempura, *sunomono* (sweet and sour cucumber slices), *tsukemono* (salted cabbage) and rice, all for $12.95. It's an ideal way to get a sampling of Teshima's delicious offerings in one shot. Their crispy, light tempura is fantastic and so is the fresh sashimi, which local fishermen bring in daily.

Teshima's also serves good ole American standbys like hamburgers, tuna sandwiches, grilled cheese and BLTs from $3.75 to $4.50, as well as lunch specials that change daily and bentos (Japanese-style box lunches to go) for $6.

Stop by and consume a piece of local Japanese history.

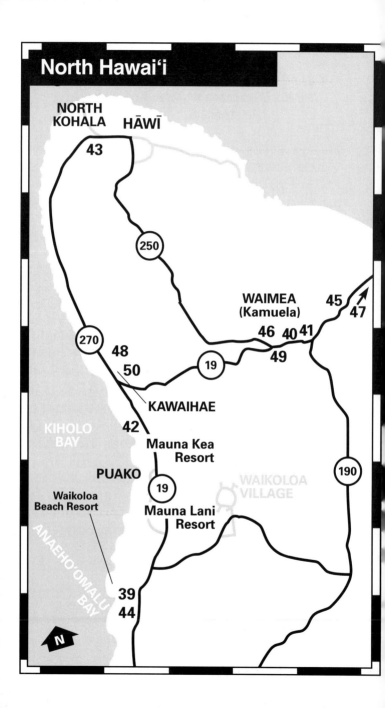

North Hawai'i

Breakfast

39. Big Island Steakhouse
40. Hawaiian Style Cafe
41. Paniolo Country Inn

Lunch

42. Hapuna Beach Grill
43. The Hawi Bakery
44. Merriman's Market Cafe
45. Tako Taco

Dinner

46. Aioli's Restaurant
47. Café Il Mondo
48. Café Pesto
49. Edelweiss
50. Seafood Bar

CUISINE	**Classic American with Big Island flair**
LOCATION	**The King's Shops at Waikoloa Beach Resort**
HOURS	**Daily, breakfast: 7 a.m. to 11:30 a.m.; lunch: 11:30 a.m. to 2:30 p.m.; dinner: 5:30 p.m. to 10 p.m.**
SEATING	**160**
PARKING	**Plenty of free parking at the King's Shops**
OPENED	**1993**
ALCOHOL	**Full bar**
PLASTIC	**Everything but A**
NOTES	**It's kid-friendly.**

39

Big Island Steakhouse
Waikoloa Beach Drive, Waikoloa Beach Resort
Telephone 886-8805

Who knew that a steakhouse would be a good spot to grab breakfast? While Steak & Eggs naturally tops the menu at Big Island Steak House, I've also tried the Original Breakfast Burrito for $5.95. It's an option for locals on their way to work, and for resort guests who don't want to sit down to a huge (and spendy) resort breakfast.

The Original Breakfast Burrito is something I might make at home on the weekend—and then skip lunch. Others might call it "hangover food." Whatever the case, eggs scrambled with fried potatoes, bacon, mushrooms, onions, peppers and cheddar cheese, rolled into a whopping flour tortilla with salsa, should set anyone straight. Another thrifty option is the Classic Egg Sandwich, two eggs over easy with bacon and cheddar on a toasted Kaiser roll, $5.25.

Families may want to consider Big Island Steakhouse for dinner. It's a rollicking family kind of place, on the Waikoloa pond, with high ceilings and a fun, casual ambience. No one cares if little Jimmy is squishing French fries in his little fists. Try the famous Baby Back Ribs. They go for $9.95 for a half-rack pupu size, or $22.95 for the whole slab, served with vegetables, baked potatoes or rice. And the house-made Hawaiian BBQ sauce is made with 42 different spices!

CUISINE	**Local-style breakfast and plate lunch**
LOCATION	**In the Hayashi Building in Waimea**
HOURS	**Monday-Friday, 7:30 a.m. to 12:45 p.m; Sunday, 7:30 a.m. to 10:30 a.m. "Come early, closed early when the food is gone." Closed Saturdays and the last Sunday and Monday of each month**
SEATING	**47**
PARKING	**Ample free parking lot outside and across the street**
OPENED	**1992**
ALCOHOL	**No**
PLASTIC	**Cash and travelers' checks only**
NOTES	**Make sure to bring your appetite—the portions are ENORMOUS!**

40

Hawaiian Style Cafe
64-1290 Kawaihae Road, Waimea
Telephone 888-4295

A staple of Hawaii's local-style cuisine is the Loco Moco, basically a hamburger patty crowned with a fried egg, served on a mattress of white rice and topped with a dollop of brown gravy. You can't say you're local unless you've consumed at least one Loco Moco.

At Hawaiian Style Cafe, you'll either become addicted to Loco Moco or swear off it for life, and I mean that as a compliment.

Here, a Loco ($6.25) is a veritable meat loaf, a one-pound patty of local grass-fed beef smothered in sautéed onions, with a local egg, loads of rice, and brown gravy. It'd satisfy a sumo wrestler with a bad case of the munchies. And if you consume the entire portion, you get pancakes on the house. I joined *Honolulu* magazine's dining editor John Heckathorn in a Hawaiian Style Loco Moco/Pancake wallow, each of us telling the other with every forkful how wrong this was for breakfast, how we usually only ate fruit and granola in the morning, and other lies. But the plain truth is a Hawaiian Style Loco Moco is wonderfully, authentically local, and it's something of a destination in itself.

Sit around the counter, where owner/head cook Mike Bendsten and his cute wife Amy are willing to answer all your dumb questions and make you feel like part of the *'ohana*, the family.

CUISINE	**Homestyle breakfast, with awesome Huevos Rancheros**
LOCATION	**At the crossroads of Waimea, near the junction of Kawaihae Road, Māmalahoa Highway and Highway 250, the Kohala Mountain Road**
HOURS	**Daily, 7 a.m. to 8:45 p.m.**
SEATING	**102**
PARKING	**Parking lot alongside the building**
OPENED	**1985**
ALCOHOL	**Full bar**
PLASTIC	**A, D, MC, V**
NOTES	**Paniolo means "Hawaiian cowboy."**

41

Paniolo Country Inn
65-1214 Lindsey Road, Waimea
Telephone 885-4377

There are at least 24 items to try on the Paniolo Country Inn breakfast menu, and I've contemplated them all, but always, faithfully, I get my tried-and-true favorite, the Huevos Rancheros with Spicy Beef. I've not found better huevos rancheros on the Big Island.

I don't know what it is, but I could eat Mexican-inspired food for every meal, and that includes breakfast. I'm in heaven at Paniolo Country Inn, which pays homage to Waimea's rich paniolo legacy. The paniolos were Spanish, Indian and Mexican cowboys brought to Hawai'i to corral and control the destructive feral cattle eating their way through native Hawaiian forests.

(The cattle were introduced to the Big Island shortly after Western contact, in 1793, by Capt. George Vancouver.) Paniolo is the Hawaiianized version of the word "Espanola," and nowadays means Hawaiian cowboy.

Eating the Huevos Rancheros with Spicy Beef ($6.50 for a full order; $3.50 for a half order) is like partaking in a delicious part of Hawaiian history. To me, the corn tortillas, salsa and beans pay tribute to the original Espanola paniolos. The spicy beef is the cattle, what the paniolos came here to control. And the fried egg and cheddar cheese are just thrown in for good measure. It's a history lesson in every bite!

CUISINE	**Beach grinds**
LOCATION	**Hāpuna Beach State Park, near the parking lot and restrooms**
HOURS	**Daily, 9 a.m. to 5 p.m.**
SEATING	**About 30 at benches; mostly take-out**
PARKING	**Hāpuna Beach State Park has free public lot**
OPENED	**2001**
ALCOHOL	**No**
PLASTIC	**None; cash is king**

Hapuna Beach Grill
62-1210 Puako Road, Hāpuna Beach
Telephone 882-0459

Hāpuna Beach is considered one of the world's best beaches, certainly the most popular on the Big Island, and it's no wonder. A long, wide ribbon of golden sand glows against the sparkling azure water, framed on each end by black lava-rock cliffs. When the surf's up, there's great body boarding and body surfing; when it's flat, snorkelers and swimmers are in heaven. Visitors and locals alike spend the entire day here—and now there's no need to pack a lunch.

Perched above the smooth sand under a shady grove of banyan trees and adjacent to the parking lot is the Hapuna Beach Grill, a beachside snack bar. Hungry beachgoers line up for the burgers, plate lunches, fries, hot dogs, salads and fish tacos. After burning off calories in the ocean, I like to replace them with a Hawaiian Ipo Salad, which is a fish taco/salad combo. For $8 you get a generous salad with citrus dressing, mandarin oranges and tropical fruit, topped with toasted coconut and macadamia nuts—plus a beer-battered fried fish filet wrapped in a flour tortilla. It's more burrito than taco, but why get technical? Beats the resort prices hands down, and it's convenient.

The best seats are the concrete park tables under the trees downhill from the snack bar but high enough above the sand to provide a magical view of beautiful Hāpuna Beach. Check it out, dude.

CUISINE	**Organic bakery and pizzeria/deli**
LOCATION	**Kohala Trade Center**
HOURS	**Daily, 11 a.m. to 8 p.m.; Wednesday, 11 a.m. to 3 p.m.**
SEATING	**15 inside/outside**
PARKING	**Public parking along the street and behind the Kohala Trade Center**
OPENED	**September 2003**
ALCOHOL	**BYOB; Kohala Spirits conveniently located next door**
PLASTIC	**V, MC**
NOTES	**Check out Cajun Saturdays for a real kick! And if you like spelt bread, call ahead to see if it's available.**

43

The Hawi Bakery
55-3419 Akoni Pule Highway, Hāwī
Telephone 889-1444

The tip of the Big Island's northwestern peninsula is Hawaii Gone Wild, where deep jungle valleys spill out onto black sand beaches and raging waterfalls and winds carve the mountainsides. It's also the end of the road, where Akoni Pule Highway stops at beautiful Pololu Valley and beach. If you haven't been there, you gotta go.

Don't bother bringing lunch. To get to Pololu, you'll pass The Hawi Bakery, located in funky little Hāwī town. Owner Gale Smart is young and passionate about his bread, particularly his sourdough, and he credits the salt air climate of seaside Hāwī for the superior quality of his homemade breads, sandwiches and pizzas. Stop by to try a thin-crust,

hand-tossed pie. I'll make the scenic drive from the Kohala Coast just for the Vegetarian, topped with veggies, an orgasmic organic homemade pesto, and goat cheese ($15 for a 12-incher). Or call ahead and have them pack a romantic deli meal for two in a deluxe Pololu Picnic Pack, which has backpack straps, and space for a bottle of wine and opener—just what newlyweds and other lovebirds need for a passionate picnic at Pololu's breathtaking black sand beach. Prices vary, and a small deposit is required.

Return the pack on your way back, and pick up a pizza for dinner while you're there. It'll be love at first bite!

CUISINE	**Mediterranean, with Hawaii regional ingredients**
LOCATION	**King's Shops at Waikoloa Beach Resort**
WEB	**www.merrimanshawaii.com**
HOURS	**Daily, 11 a.m. to 9:30 p.m.; lunch: 11 a.m. to 2 p.m.; bar pupu menu: 2 p.m. to 5 p.m.; dinner: 5 to 9:30 p.m**
SEATING	**115**
PARKING	**Plenty of free parking at the King's Shops**
OPENED	**November 2003**
ALCOHOL	**Full bar, fine wine**
PLASTIC	**A, MC, V**
NOTES	**Visit Merriman's Restaurant in Waimea for lunch or dinner—it's not as thrifty, but it has really great food.**

44

Merriman's Market Cafe
250 Waikoloa Beach Drive, Waikoloa Beach Resort
Telephone 886-1700

I've been a fan of Chef Peter Merriman's for years. His name and fame are synonymous with Hawaii Regional Cuisine. His upscale restaurants in Waimea and Maui are top-notch, but not thrifty. But Chef Peter's latest venture, Merriman's Market Cafe at Waikoloa's King's Shops, is perfectly located for resort guests, resort workers and any-one looking for delicious and exciting food showcasing the best locally grown ingredients—and it's affordable!

At Merriman's Market Cafe, even the simplest foods become cuisine. French fries are called *Pommes Frittes* and are served with housemade ketchup and aioli, irresistible and only $2.95. I always have the locally grown Roasted Beet and Ricotta Salad, tossed with fresh mint and arugula in Champagne vinaigrette—a winner

at $8.25—and a small plate of housemade Hummus with Warm Pita ($5.95). Healthy, simple and delicious.

The menu here is Mediterranean, with an emphasis on Italian, but there are no boundaries. There are wonderfully worldly sandwiches for lunch like the Grilled Eggplant and Roasted Red Pepper Sandwich ($8.95), served on your choice of artisan bread. It's enlivened by Hāmākua goat cheese and spicy harissa, a zesty North African condiment made from oil, chilies, garlic, cumin and other aromatic ingredients.

King's Shops is a nice selection of stores, from upscale boutiques like Indochine to a ukulele dealer, a Starbucks, even a Macy's. Merriman's Market Cafe is a welcome addition.

CUISINE	**Mexican-American**
LOCATION	**Cook's Corner, at the Kamamalu Street stoplight**
HOURS	**Daily, 7 a.m. to 9 p.m. (call to make sure!)**
SEATING	**50 indoors, 8 outdoors**
PARKING	**Parking lot next to building**
OPENED	**1999, moved to new location, 2005, and will reopen there in late April or early May**
ALCOHOL	**They're in the process of applying for a beer and wine license.**
PLASTIC	**A, JCB, MC, V**
NOTES	**There's a drive-up window for breakfast; for lunch and dinner, call ahead for quick-pickup takeout.**

Tako Taco
64-1066 Māmalahoa Highway, Waimea
Telephone 887-1717

I've eaten at Tako Taco a dozen times, but I've never had a *tako* (octopus) taco. They used to have a tako taco but found out it makes a better mascot. It's just too darn chewy.

What I like is the healthy Tofu Taco for $3.25, layered with their fabulous house-made black beans, Monterey jack cheese and shredded cabbage. Tofu is a great alternative to meat, and Tako Taco does a great job of turning tofu into a flavorful treat by marinating it in a special grilled-tomato ranchero sauce.

If I'm really hungry, I order the Special Veggie Burrito for $5.75. It's a giant flour tortilla rolled with rice, black beans, cheese, slaw, guacamole and a hot or mild pico de gallo tomato salsa. I often grab two of these on Fridays after work and bring one home to Mountain View for Steve. If I'm famished, I swallow my pride, hope no one I know passes me on the road, and somehow wolf mine down in the car. It's not a pretty sight, but the evidence is long gone by the time I hit Honokaʻa. Steve reports that his burrito tastes just as good two hours later.

For the seriously thrifty diners, Tako Taco also offers a side of beans and rice for a mere $1.50. Their pinto beans are every bit as delicious as their black beans. See you there!

(Tako Taco recently moved; the photo opposite is of the former location.)

CUISINE	Eclectic American, featuring locally grown products
LOCATION	Opelo Plaza, near Merriman's
HOURS	Tuesday-Thursday, 11 a.m. to 8 p.m.; Friday and Saturday, 11 a.m. to 9 p.m.; closed Sunday and Monday
SEATING	30
PARKING	Ample parking in front
OPENED	August 1997
ALCOHOL	BYOB; no corkage fee
PLASTIC	V, MC, D
NOTES	Reservations are recommended. Aioli's specializes in tender, young New Zealand lamb specials. Although we've not tried the lamb here, there are reports that a small revolt erupted when the owners took it off the menu. It's back on.

46

Aioli's Restaurant
65-1158 Māmalahoa Highway, Waimea
Telephone 885-6325

This homey little nook is easily overlooked by visitors. It's tucked in the back of Opelo Plaza, almost in the shadow of its highly acclaimed neighbor, Merriman's. But Big Island locals, 80 percent of the clientele, relish great food for a fair price, and they keep Aioli's busy five nights a week.

Named for a French concoction of mayonnaise, olive oil and loads of fresh garlic, Aioli's is a garlic lover's paradise. Chef/owner Jerry Mills changes the menu every three weeks, but he always finds a way to slip garlic into the mix, whether it's whole cloves stuffed into tender lamb, garlic-laced mashed potatoes or perhaps a creamy soup.

It's not quite *everywhere*: My co-worker Rae and I revved up with a garlic-free Hāmākua Goat Cheese and Shiitake Mushroom Paté ($4.95), presented in three bite-size pastry shells. Recipe, please! Next came a Weed Salad, with organic (and completely legal!) mizuna and arugula—virtually free of garlic until we anointed it with house-made creamy peppercorn garlic dressing. Finally, some dressing to get excited about! Then, since our men were away and we didn't have to worry about our breath, we dove into a bowl of deliciously pungent thick Garlic Cream Soup, dunking chunks of homemade roll slathered with the namesake aioli.

We were blissed out on soup, salad and mushroom paté, but the homemade *Lilikoi* (passion fruit) Cheesecake (see Sweet Endings) was over-the-top dessert heaven. I'm not supposed to have sweets anymore, but this was worth the calories!

CUISINE	**Homestyle Italian, featuring a stone pizza oven**
LOCATION	**On Honoka'a's main drag, makai side**
HOURS	**Monday-Saturday, 10 a.m. to 9 p.m.; closed Sundays**
SEATING	**About 30 inside and outside**
PARKING	**Ample free parking along Mamane Street**
OPENED	**1996**
ALCOHOL	**BYOB; $2/table corkage fee, or $4 for 5 or more people**
PLASTIC	**No, cash and travelers checks only**

47

Café Il Mondo
45-3626 Mamane Street, Honoka'a
775-7711

If you've ever wondered what to eat in Honoka'a besides malasadas, that question can be answered at Café Il Mondo. This delightful sidewalk pizzeria and coffee bar occupies a building on Honoka'a's main drag, Mamane Street, just a few doors down from the People's Theater, home of the annual Hamakua Music Festival. At Cafe Il Mondo, there is indoor and outdoor seating, and often times, live music. Pretty hip for a small former sugar town like Honoka'a.

Steve and I walked in on a busy night but got a table right away. We planned to dance at the festival later, so we decided to split a generous Greek Salad, with fresh spinach, Feta cheese, tomatoes, Kalamata olives and

garlic bread for $7.25. It was a fantastic salad, but those home-baked aromas were getting to us. A golden calzone was carried to a table nearby, and that did it—we found ourselves digging into a massive Italian sausage calzone ($8.25). A calzone is a pizza turnover stuffed with marinara and mozzarella cheese and, in this case, sausage, olives, onions and mushrooms. Phenomenal! The Café Il Mondo chef makes the dough, pesto and pizza sauces, focaccia, sandwiches and calzones fresh daily.

After dinner, sip a latte ($2.75) at the beautiful 1924 bar made from native Hawaiian koa wood. It might be enough to get you on the dance floor.

CUISINE	**Creative Island cuisine**
LOCATION	**Kawaihae Harbor Center**
WEB	**www.cafepesto.com**
HOURS	**Sunday-Thursday, 11 a.m. to 9 p.m.; Friday and Saturday, 11 a.m. to 10 p.m.**
SEATING	**100**
PARKING	**Parking lot, or along Kawaihae**
OPENED	**1988**
ALCOHOL	**Full bar**
PLASTIC	**All cards**
NOTE	**There's another Café Pesto on Kamehameha Avenue in downtown Hilo; their number is 969-6640.**

48

Café Pesto
Kawaihae Harbor Center, Kawaihae
Telephone 882-1071

Kawaihae's Café Pesto is a Big Island institution, conveniently located near the luxury resorts of the Kohala Coast. The menu features plenty of Hawai'i regional cuisine, fresh fish and eclectic pizza—it's hardly thrifty—but I can lead you to the promised land of less-expensive and equally delicious items.

Take the Blue Caesar Salad ($5.50). Here we have crisp hearts of Kiwano Farms romaine, tossed with Gorgonzola cheese and anchovy-buttered croutons. Absolutely luscious! Combine that with the Asian Pacific Crab Cakes, which are seared light and crispy with a honey-miso vinaigrette sauce and pickled cucumber ($12.95, but it's a good-sized appetizer), and you have a light gourmet meal.

Café Pesto is less expensive at lunch, but I like to go with friends after work for early dinner and share everything. We get an order of the Free Range Chicken and Forest Mushroom Risotto ($18.95), which is sliced chicken breast, Oriental mushrooms and bell peppers over creamy saffron rice; plus a large Blue Caesar and at least one of Café Pesto's outstanding pizzas, which range from $8.50 to $10.95 for a 9-incher. I love the Oriental, which has fresh basil pesto, roasted garlic, sun-dried tomatoes and Japanese eggplant (the Oriental part), $10.95.

Save room for dessert: the hot Keanakolu Fresh Apple Crisp ($5.95) and a cup of Lion coffee ($1.95) will give you energy for the rest of the night.

CUISINE	**European/Continental**
LOCATION	**Downtown Waimea, across from Kamuela Inn**
HOURS	**Lunch: 11:30 a.m. to 1:30 p.m.; dinner: 5 to 8:30-ish. Closed Sunday and Monday**
SEATING	**70**
PARKING	**Plenty**
OPENED	**1983**
ALCOHOL	**Full bar; the only place serving Erdinger on tap on the Big Island**
PLASTIC	**V, MC**

49

Edelweiss
65-1299 Kawaihae Road, Waimea
Telephone 885-6800

I'm constantly amazed by the diversity of the Big Island: its people, its climate, its food. When I ducked into Edelweiss on a drizzly, nippy Waimea evening, its warm, rustic walls of silver oak and its low-lit tables reminded me of an Alpine lodge. Just another day in paradise!

I'd heard good things about the restaurant and its owner/chef Hans-Peter Hager, but I doubted his Continental, German-influenced menu would be thrifty enough for this book. After all, most dinner entrées fall into the $20-$27 range. Flip to the back page of the menu, though, and you'll find the "Light Dinner" section. Here I discovered bratwurst, the classic German grilled sausage, served with fresh rolls, sauerkraut and warm German potato salad, for $10.50. I cut it in half and enjoyed each savory, juicy slice with a sip of sweet Riesling ($5/glass). I pushed the second half aside, trying not to overeat, but it refused to be ignored—its smooth texture and grill-marked casing challenged me to finish it off with a pint of Erdinger, a dynamite German heffeweizen ($5.25). German perfection. (Note to self: listen to the bratwurst.) Afterwards, the chef insisted I try his homemade chocolate Bavarian pie ($4; see Sweet Endings). Definitely save room for dessert.

I left absolutely smitten with Edelweiss, and I'll return. If I'd skipped the booze, my dinner, dessert, tax and tip would have only been about $20. "*Mahlzeit!*"

CUISINE   **Seafood and eclectic American**

LOCATION   **Kawaihae, across the street from several huge fuel silos**

HOURS   **Lunch: daily, 11:30 a.m. to 2:30 p.m.; dinner: Sunday-Thursday, 2:30 p.m. to 10:30 p.m.; Friday and Saturday, 2:30 p.m. to 11:30 p.m.; bar open to 2 a.m. seven nights a week**

SEATING   **80**

PARKING   **Ample parking**

OPENED   **May 2002**

ALCOHOL   **Full bar**

PLASTIC   **MC, V**

NOTES   **Every day from 2:30 to 5:30 p.m. is happy hour. Import draft beers, well drinks and well margaritas are $3 each.**

50

Seafood Bar
61-3642 Kawaihae Road, Kawaihae
Telephone 880-9393

Employees of the Kohala Coast resorts, as well as other locals, belly up to Seafood Bar for their *pau hana* (after work) cocktails and a quick pupu (appetizer), and resort guests are following suit.

Somewhat close to most of the major resorts but out of the resort-price zone with its Kawaihae address, the relatively new Seafood Bar has already won a devoted local following. With its tight little menu of tasty, affordable pupus like Coconut Shrimp ($6.50), Smoked Marlin-Stuffed Mushrooms ($5.95) and fresh sashimi ($12.95), this snazzy tiki hut lives up to its name, and it's easy to see why visitors are among the clientele: the prices are decidedly unresort-like.

My hotel pals and I welcome the weekend with ice-cold Coronas ($3/bottle at happy hour) and a couple of appetizers. My favorite grinds are the Spinach Dinner Salad ($5.95) and the Spicy Soy Beans ($2.50). But my favorite aspects of Seafood Bar are its décor and laid-back Polynesian ambience. Even though massive fuel silos block the view to the ocean, the owners make sure you remember you're in Hawai'i. Lauhala mats cover the walls, along with surfing memorabilia and Don Ho album covers. The large glass doors are etched with a tiki, and a huge ship's wheel steers you toward the bar. Ahoy!

Insider's tip: *Hawai'i Island Journal* dining editor Brian Berry chose Seafood Bar as the Big Island's top bar for 2004.

Sweet Endings
A Dozen of the Big Island's Best, Least Expensive Sweets

Aioli's Lilikoi Cheesecake, $3,75 a slice, $42 for the whole thing. *(Made with locally grown lilikoi, a.k.a. passionfruit, it offers a perfect sweet/tart balance in every creamy bite.)* 65-1158 Māmalahoa Highway, Waimea

Arnie's Clubhouse Restaurant Frozen Grasshopper Pie, $5 slice. *(Crème de Menthe ice cream laced with frozen vanilla mousse in an Oreo-cookie crust, topped with chocolate sauce, is sure to cure any golfer's handicap.)* Hāpuna Golf Course, 62-100 Kaunaoa Dr., Kohala Coast

Big Island Candies Chocolate-dipped original shortbread cookies, $8.75 for a lovely gold box of 15 individually wrapped treats. *(The retail candy factory is a must-visit in Hilo. My faraway friends insist I bring these when I visit. As addictive as heroin, but less expensive.)* 585 Hinano St., Hilo

Big Island Grill Flourless Chocolate Cake, $4. *(Served warm with a raspberry sauce and ice cream. All desserts are homemade and broke da mout'!)* 75-5702 Kuakini Hwy., Kailua-Kona

Café Pesto Can't decide? Get both! Warm coconut tart, $4.95. *(Sinful, with a sweet créme anglaise.)* Also to die for: the Hot Keanakolu Apple Crisp, $5.95 a piece. *(Baked fresh apples with a topping of—what else?—macadamia nut crumbs.)* Kawaihae Shopping Center, Kawaihae, or 308 Kamehameha Ave., Hilo.

Hilo Bay Café Fresh fruit tart, $6. *(Chef Josh imports fresh berries from California for his homemade tart, and tops it with a delightful vanilla crème anglaise.)* 315 Makaala Street, Hilo

Kozmic Cones Chocolate-dipped soft serve vanilla cone, $1.70 for a small, $1.90 for a medium cone. *(Who needs Dairy Queen?)* 317 Waianuenue Ave., Hilo

Mountainview Bakery Original Stone Cookies, $4.50/dozen. *(The original cookies are so hard they're like Milk Bones for humans, but they taste more like fortune cookies. Also available at KTA Superstores and Longs Drugs.)* 18-1319 Old Volcano Hwy., Mountainview

Naalehu Fruit Stand Homemade macadamia nut shortbread, $1 a square. *(Homemade with macadamia nuts, mac nut butter and out-of-this-world delicious!)* 19-1319 Old Volcano Hwy., Nā'ālehu

Nasturtium Café Macadamia Nut Tart, $6.50. *(Made with whole, locally grown mac nuts and natural Stevia sweetener, it's what the late local comedian Rap Reiplinger would describe as "not too sweet, not too rancid, but jus' right!")* 79-7491 B. Māmalahoa Hwy., Kealakekua.

Tex Drive In & Restaurant Homemade malasadas, 88 cents each, $9/dozen. *(A local favorite, malasadas are deep-fried, "hole-free" Portuguese doughnuts sand-blasted in fine white sugar. Go for the originals.)* 45-690 Pakalana St., Honokaa, or 96-3183 Pikake St., Pahala

Tropical Dreams/Hilo Homemade Ice Cream $2.25+ for a cone; prices vary by location. *(Creamy confections made on the Big Island. The cherry vanilla is an ice cream dream!)* There are eight locations on the Big Island: Kohala Coffee Mill, Akoni Pule Highway, Hāwī; Waipio Vallery Art Works, 48-5416 Kukuihaele Rd., Kukuihaele; Aloha Outpost, 15-2937 Pāhoa Village Road, Pāhoa; Antique Arts, 81-6593 Māmalahoa Highway, Kealakekua; Daylight Donuts, 78-6831 Ali'i Dr., Kailua-Kona; Down to Surf, 1477 Kalanianaole Ave., Hilo; Hilo Homemade Downtown Store, 41 Waianuenue Ave., Hilo; Simply Natural, 45-3625 Mamane St., Honoka'a.

Glossary

'ahi	yellowfin tuna
aioli	garlic mayonnaise
'awa	kava, mildly narcotic root made into a drink
bento	Japanese-style box lunch
daikon	mild white Japanese radish
haloumi	Middle-Eastern string cheese
kaiware	radish sprouts
kalua pig	pork roasted in an underground oven
katsu	Japanese-style breaded, fried chicken or pork
keiki	child, children
kiawe	algaroba tree, mesquite
lanai	porch or deck
lilikoi	passionfruit
Loco Moco	rice topped with a hamburger patty, a fried egg, and gravy
malasada	Portuguese doughnut
manapua	Chinese steamed bun, often filled with roast pork
miso	fermented soybean paste
mizuna	Japanese salad vegetable

natto	fermented soybeans
noni	Hawaiian fruit with health-giving properties
ono	mackerel
'ono	delicious
opihi	small, round Hawaiian shellfish
ponzu	Japanese citrus sauce
pūpū	appetizer
saimin	thin noodles in broth
sashimi	raw fish
sunomono	sweet-sour cucumber
sushi	rice, fish, vegetables, etc., rolled in seaweed
taro	purple-gray starchy root, a Polynesian staple
tempeh	meat-like soybean product
tempura	Japanese-style battered, deep-fried shrimp or vegetables
tsukemono	salted cabbage
udon	thick Japanese wheat-paste noodles
'ulu	breadfruit
ume	pickled plum
wasabi	hot green Japanese radish

About the Author

Jessica Ferracane grew up in Hawaiʻi and was a Maui-based journalist before changing lanes—and islands—to pursue a career in public relations. As a journalist, she wrote dining reviews for several magazines and guidebooks. She is currently the Director of Public Relations at The Fairmont Orchid, Hawaiʻi, located on the Big Island's sun-soaked Kohala Coast. She would like readers to know that she personally sampled the food at each of the 50 Thrifty restaurants at least once, paying for almost all of her meals out-of-pocket and packing on twenty pounds in the name of research! When she's not working or checking out the latest restaurant, Jessica can be found in the jungle of East Hawaiʻi with her husband and their three dogs, wondering what's for dinner.

Index

Order More Hawai'i Dining Guides
from Watermark Publishing

Watermark Publishing
1088 Bishop Street, Suite 310
Honolulu, Hawai'i 96813

Toll-free 1-866-900-BOOK
sales@bookshawaii.net

Name _____ Phone _____

Address _____

City _____ State _____ Zip _____

TITLE	PRICE	QTY.	
50 Thrifty Maui Restaurants	$6.95 x	_____ =	$ _____
The Puka Guide	$8.95 x	_____ =	$ _____
The Okazu Guide	$8.95 x	_____ =	$ _____
The Omiyage Guide	$8.95 x	_____ =	$ _____
Shipping & handling (USPS Priority Mail)*			$ _____
TOTAL ORDER			**$ _____**

❑ Check enclosed, payable to Watermark Publishing

❑ Charge my credit card ❑ Visa ❑ MC ❑ Amex
❑ Discover ❑ Diner's ❑ Carte Blanche

Card no. _____ Exp. date _____

Signature Required _____

* *$2 each up to 10 copies, $1 each 11-50 copies, call for more than 50*